ULTIMATE THINGS

*An Orthodox Christian Perspective
on the End Times*

by Dennis Eugene Engleman

CONCILIAR PRESS
Ben Lomond, California

ULTIMATE THINGS
© 1995 Dennis Eugene Engleman
All rights reserved
Printed in the United States of America

Conciliar Press
P.O. Box 76, Ben Lomond, California 95005-0076

Library of Congress Cataloging-in-Publication Data

Engleman, Dennis Eugene, 1948–
    Ultimate things : an Orthodox Christian
perspective on the end times / by Dennis Eugene
Engleman.
        p.   cm.
    Includes bibliographical references and index.
    ISBN 0-9622713-9-X
    1. End of the world. 2. Eschatology. 3. Orthodox
Eastern Church--Doctrines. I. Title.
BT876.E54   1995
236'.9--dc20   95-24936
                                                          CIP

Table of Contents

Foreword

The manuscript of *Ultimate Things* was sent to me for review some months ago. I was excited to see that someone had taken pains to approach this critically important but difficult subject—the end times, the Return of Christ, and the need for Christians to prepare themselves for these events—from an Orthodox perspective.

I found the book interesting, sobering, and inspiring. It addresses a very complex and confusing subject in a way that is simple, clear, well-written, and basically sound. I am both instructed and encouraged by having read it. I was glad to see that the author presents his treatise as one attempt to interpret the apocalyptic passages in the Bible from an Orthodox perspective, and not as a presentation of *"the* Orthodox teaching." On the other hand, he also avoids the pitfall of personal speculation.

The author deals competently and faithfully with several points which distinguish an Orthodox perspective on the end times from the teachings of other Christian confessions. I especially appreciated his interpretation of the teaching about the "rapture," and his identification of the millennium of Christ's rule on earth with the age of the Church. While I would take issue with the author on certain points (such as his view of the last Russian tsar as the one who "restrains the mystery of lawlessness," as well as his interpretation of catacomb Christianity), I found much to be convincing and in accordance with both the biblical evidence and the teaching of the Holy Fathers. Especially helpful is his depiction of the Antichrist as a human being with certain discernible characteristics.

Ultimate Things is a clarion call for Orthodox Christians to remain true to Christ and the Church in the days ahead. Personally, I found myself challenged by its message. Orthodox Christians, who are aware of each other and are mystically connected historically and structurally through the Holy Spirit, have plenty to think about here!

For non-Orthodox, this book should be even more challenging and thought-provoking. For those who have found themselves nearly pulled to pieces by the morass of conflicting modern interpretations of the apocalyptic Scriptures, here is an opportunity to confront some of the traditional teachings of those who seek to represent the mind of the historic Church of Jesus Christ. The author attempts to clear away the cobwebs of multitudinous private interpretations so that the historic light of God's Truth can shine clearly once again. Christians who wish to be prepared for their Lord's Return cannot afford to settle for less.

May we be up to the demands of staying faithful to the Lord as we continue on to that great and dreadful day of His Coming in glory!

> —Father Thomas Hopko, Dean
> Saint Vladimir's Orthodox Seminary
> Crestwood, New York

Things fall apart; the centre cannot hold;
Mere anarchy is loosed upon the world,
The blood-dimmed tide is loosed, and everywhere
The ceremony of innocence is drowned;
The best lack all conviction, while the worst
Are full of passionate intensity.

Surely some revelation is at hand;
Surely the Second Coming is at hand.

—William Butler Yeats, "The Second Coming"

A prudent man foresees evil and hides himself;
The simple pass on and are punished.
           —Proverbs 27:12

Chapter 1

The Last Christians

Christianity, as a spirit . . . is withdrawing from the midst of humanity, leaving it [the world] to its fall.
        —*Saint Ignatius Brianchaninov*

"The modern age has ended," declared Czech Republic President Vaclav Havel in 1994. "Today, many things indicate that we are going through a transitional period, when it seems that something is on the way out and something else is painfully being born. It is as if something were crumbling, decaying, and exhausting itself, while something else, still indistinct, were arising from the rubble."[1]

Havel's assessment is seconded by others who sense that this age has reached a long-awaited conclusion. History has been fulfilled, they assert, and what will follow is beyond the limits of prior human experience. James Davidson, author of *The Great Reckoning*, said that we stand at "the end of the modern world and the beginning of whatever we will eventually call this new world that is coming to be."[2]

The end of the age . . . the end of the world . . these are heady concepts. They invoke, even with the qualifier "modern," an idea which has reverberated throughout sacred history like a distantly approaching thunderclap—a premonition of dread to generation who hoped they would not live to experience it. And now this mysterious event is being discussed almost casually in political and economic circles.

There is a growing perception that humanity's great saga has reached some point of finality, or at least final transformation. Contemporary commentators are uncertain, however, about the significance of this point and what may lie beyond it. Attempts at explanation are typically groping and futile, based on linear Cartesian/Kantian models, within which no "end" is really plausible.

Yet few have turned for understanding to Orthodox Christianity, the only authentic interpreter of this period. Instead, the "religion of man" in its various mutations is sweeping civilization like an epidemic; faith in humanity has at last rendered faith in God nearly impossible, or at least heretical. Jesus Christ is considered an outgrown concept—a mere sentimental pacifier for the immature or superstitious. "Christianity as a whole," writes Archimandrite Constantine of Holy Trinity Monastery in Jordanville, New York, "is outrightly declared to be a historical category that has outlived itself."[3]

Man now views himself not as an integral (though lowly) member of the heavenly plan, but as one standing alone and accidental in a totally material cosmo

does not believe in God, so he entertains neither
e of heaven nor fear of hell. Furthermore, he con-
rs his secular and atheistic attitude to be the best
ence of maturity, as contemporary author Thomas
nar noted: "The conviction has grown that man has
red the 'last period'—the period of mankind's matu-
—when the concept of God may be discarded."[4]

et God has not been discarded so much as co-
d. Man is no longer content to be merely man
n though he has conspicuously failed to meet the
demands of the job)—he wants to be "God"!
sidering himself inherently divine, a god-in-the-
ing, he now tolerates no restrictions to his will and
sure. Through science and magic he forces the
rs of the universe, especially those which were
nerly barred by faith. Everything is possible; he will
s he pleases, for he has adopted Nietzsche's nihilis-
redo: "All is false—everything is allowed!"[5]

But just as the world is within man's grasp, it seems
e *ending!* And having abandoned faith and truth,
cannot honestly face the crisis. As contemporary
istic scholar Father Seraphim Rose lamented, "He
able, or unwilling, to think in terms of ends, of
nate things. The thirst for absolute truth has van-
d; it has been swallowed up in worldliness."[6]

A great chasm looms ahead and the light which had
led man's previous steps does not extend into the
. Suddenly, from the dread darkness, the distorted
ister he so carelessly and shamelessly enticed begins
merge . . .

"What we see terrifies us, for we see the end [of] world, an apocalypse," wrote historian William I[r]win Thompson; "and this *is* an apocalypse, for it is [the] ending of ourselves and the old world we made ourselves to be comfortable in. . . . Church and uni[ver]sity, government and art, all those institutions [that] were once pillars of civilization and carriers of [the] Divine Word, no longer seem to be filled with [the] holiness, wisdom, and power they once had."[7]

Like a sun sinking into feverish dusk, the "worl[d] made for ourselves" is collapsing into the greate[st] nights. For, as the record of history testifies, [a] creation, when devoid of the light of Christ, is a ho[use] of unmitigated darkness. Like the demons who te[mpt] and then accuse those they've tempted, Nietz[sche] mocked man's infernal predicament: "Do ye also [want] a light, ye most concealed, strongest and most [un]daunted men of the blackest midnight?"[8]

The conventional moral order, based on a reco[gni]tion of divine principles, has been rejected. A mal[evo]lent "nothing" has replaced them. And in this abse[nce] of holiness, wisdom, and godly power, only "noth[ing]" can be accomplished, for as Jesus said, "the nig[ht] coming when no one can work" (John 9:4).

Indeed, people cannot even *remain* in this dark[ness] and still retain their humanity! For nihilism, the n[oth]ingness to which this post-Christian world has b[een] reduced, cannot tolerate the reality of *Man,* wh[o is] made in the image of *God.* Thus, in seeking only h[im]self at the cost of Christ, modern man loses prec[ious]

self. Yet this stark and ruthless bargain goes un-
led by those who must ante up the price.

ather Seraphim Rose suggested truth might be
ned as "knowledge of the beginning and end of
gs."[9] Yet in these benighted times, the "end of the
ld" has been demeaned to a mere sound-bite. The
1 has been emasculated and sedated—civilized and
le non-threatening . . . or so it is hoped. Stripped of
itual significance, it has been packaged as a mere
orical interlude, albeit a potentially traumatic one.
Yet the reality of this period is far more awesome
1 the mind of man can yet conceive. It is an occasion
1e gravest spiritual struggle for the soul of human-
and a prelude to the Return of Jesus Christ. The
1 Himself referred to it often: "Lo, I am with you
1ys, even to the end of the age [or world]" (Matthew
20). And in spite of all professions to the contrary,
e times cannot be apprehended—or survived—
:t from the authentic Christian Faith, from which
r derive their true meaning and most appropriate
1e: the end times.

is Generation

saved from this perverse generation," Saint Peter
orted Christians on the day of Pentecost (Acts 2:40).
wise, the Lord warned that "this generation will by no
1ns pass away till all these things take place" (Matthew
34). The things He referred to were the events of the
days, and the generation is our own. Saint John
ysostom (d. 407) stressed that the Lord spoke "not of

the generation then living, but of that of the believer

Christians concerned with being saved "from perverse generation" are in a unique position. world in which they live has reached an impasse: it completed its rejection of Christ and declared the of normal—that is, Christian—history. Any belie left in these "post-Christian" times might well be c sidered the "last Christians." Yet there is a deeper t to such a label, for the eschatology upon which th believers' faith hinges makes it clear that they ma fact have no spiritual descendants!

So skewed is worldly society, with its humani and atheistic ideals, that strange and frightening oc rences have become the norm. Standards have becc inverted—bad is considered good, right is consid wrong. "Woe to those," Isaiah wailed of us, "who evil good, and good evil; who put darkness for li and light for darkness; who put bitter for sweet, sweet for bitter" (Isaiah 5:20).

The distinction between virtue and vice has di peared; values have been relativized into oblivion. result, noble aspirations are undermined or condem deviant conduct rewarded and congratulated. The (of the living is "dead," and into His corpse the voo practitioners of the world stick pins in order to ca lethal and hellish curse upon mankind.

A World in Chains
Conceptions about the end times abound in literat and the term has acquired a mystique which gener

ds its users as starry-eyed dreamers far removed
1 mundane reality. Yet this period, which, accord-
o some Orthodox thinkers' interpretation of bibli-
nd patristic teaching, started early in the twentieth
ury (see Chapter 6), has initiated earth-shaking
1ges which are very real.

World slavery is materializing before our eyes like
nshrouding fog. Daily, chains are forged and the
s snapped tight by those who will wear them. Yet
all will be enslaved, for Jesus promised, "You shall
w the truth, and the truth shall make you free"
n 8:32).

or this reason, those who will deny men freedom
attempt to deny them truth. Yet Truth can never
ılly repressed, for it is not a fact or dogma, but a
on. Even if all books are burned and memories
terated, "neither death nor life, nor angels nor
cipalities nor powers, nor things present nor things
ome, nor height nor depth, nor *any other created*
g, shall be able to separate us from the love of God
ch is in Christ Jesus our Lord" (Romans 8:38, 39,
hasis added).

d Times Guidance

ertheless, it is clear that the end times are the most
cult of all times. And because of this, the last
istians have been given a great deal of guidance and
. The Old and New Testaments are replete with
ructions and warnings concerning the last days.
evers are taught what to watch for, what to listen

17

for; they are advised what to say and do about v
they see and hear. The Lord expects His followers t
alert to the signs He has given, so as not to be t
unawares. Like insider traders capitalizing on clan
tine investment knowledge, they are to anticipate
most momentous of all "market" fluctuations,
move their treasure to safety. This will enable ther
live, even in history's final moments, as wise stewar
their Master's wealth. "Blessed is that servant," J
said, "whom his master will find so doing wher
comes" (Luke 12:43).

In a word, Christians are counseled to *get re*
"Guard thyself then, O man; thou hast the sign
Antichrist," wrote Saint Cyril of Jerusalem in the fo
century; "and remember them not only thyself,
impart them also freely to all."[11]

What are believers to get ready for? Most im
tantly, for the dread and awesome judgment of Ch
But also, to survive the onslaught of Antichrist as
utterly depraved being seduces and destroys the wo
For it is *only* the last Christians who will survive h

Yet "survival" does not here mean preserving
for many will be called to die for the Truth. What n
survive is faith in God! Believers must teach t
children to discern right from wrong, and to
Christ more than earthly existence. "If thou hast a c
according to the flesh, admonish him of this no
instructed Saint Cyril of Jerusalem. "If thou hast be
ten one through catechizing, put him also on his gu
lest he receive the false one as the True."[12]

These preparations can proceed discreetly. The last Christians need not showcase their efforts. On the contrary, they should do everything possible to build strength secretly, without the enemy's knowledge. "Our times, above all," counseled Father Seraphim Rose, "call for *humble and quiet labors,* with love and sympathy for other strugglers on the path of the Orthodox spiritual life and a deep resolve that does not become discouraged because the atmosphere is unfavorable. . . . If we do this, even in our terrible times, we may have hope—in God's mercy—of the salvation of our souls."[13]

Out of "love and sympathy for other strugglers on the path of the Orthodox spiritual life," this volume has been prepared. Its goal is to present an Orthodox perspective and chronology of the end times, based on the writings of the Church Fathers, for the sake of those unacquainted with these important teachings. While modern interpreters have also been consulted, speculation and subjective opinion have been avoided in order to let the true patristic guidance be heard. For it is the voices of the Church Fathers, always in harmony with the biblical precepts of Jesus Christ and His Apostles, which can illuminate our steps even in these confused and contradictory times.

---

[1] *Utne Reader,* January-February 1995, p. 53 (recorded on the occasion of Havel's receiving the Philadelphia Liberty Medal at Independence Hall).

[2] *Forecasts & Forewarnings,* January 2, 1995, p. 7.

[3] *Ecumenism, Communism, and Apostasy: The Spiritual State of the Contemporary World,* p. 17.

[4] *Utopia: The Perennial Heresy,* p. 117.

[5] *The Will to Power,* Vol. II in *The Complete Works of Friedrich Nietzsche,* p. 102.

[6] Eugene (Fr. Seraphim) Rose, *Nihilism: The Root of the Revolution of the Modern Age,* p. 31.

[7] *Darkness and Scattered Light,* pp. 35, 37.

[8] *The Will to Power,* p. 432.

[9] *Nihilism,* p. 35.

[10] "Homily LXXVII," P. Schaff & H. Wace, eds., *A Select Library of Nicene and Post-Nicene Fathers of the Christian Church,* Vol. X, p. 462.

[11] "Catechetical Lectures," Lecture XV, part 18, in *Nicene and Post-Nicene Fathers,* Vol. VII, p. 110.

[12] *Ibid.*

[13] Quoted in Monk Damascene Christensen, *Not of This World: The Life and Teaching of Fr. Seraphim Rose,* p. 633.

Chapter 2

Why Do You Stand Gazing?

*Is the modern world really anything whatever
but a direct denial of all traditional truth? It
wears every disguise, often the most unexpected,
to avoid being recognized for what it is, and
even to pass itself off as the very opposite of what
it is.*

—*Rene Guenon*

"Why do you stand gazing up into heaven?" With
these words angels accosted Jesus' stupefied disciples as
their Lord ascended from the earth. "This same Jesus,"
they said, "who was taken up from you into heaven,
will so come in like manner as you saw Him go into
heaven" (Acts 1:11).

The disciples' answer, if they gave one, has not been
preserved. But it may well have been, "We want to see
our Lord come back!" And like those first Apostles,
Christians have been "gazing up into heaven" for the
past two millennia, anticipating His Return.

Christ's Second Coming has been announced by
the lips of angels. Although the Lord never revealed
when this would happen, He spoke of many signs

which would indicate the nearness of the event, and promised to be with His children until then: "I am with you always, even to the end of the age" (Matthew 28:20).

The Lord's past Resurrection and His future Return have defined the real milestones of mankind's history, and given a framework of meaning to all lesser occurrences. As a prelude to the end times, Saint John called this entire period between Christ's First and Second Comings the "last hour": "Little children, it is the last hour" (1 John 2:18).

Setting Dates

Over the years many attempts have been made to determine the actual date of Christ's Return. Joachim of Fiore published his expectation of A.D. 1260, based on a cycle of forty-two generations from Adam to Christ, and the supposition of forty-two more from Christ to the Second Coming. In the fifteenth century, Cardinal Nicholas of Cusa affirmed that the world would not outlast 1734. The Anabaptist Melchior Hoffman announced the Second Coming for the year 1553. The Quaker James Milner expected the world's end in December of 1652. In 1730, Abbe Etimare, a Jansenist, declared that the war of the Beast had begun and that it would end in 1733. In 1761, George Bell, a Methodist, warned his parishioners that the world would end in 1763. In 1758, Shaker Ann Lee claimed to be the female Messiah. In 1786, another Shaker, Jemima Wilkinson, insisted that *she* was the Messiah.

William Miller caused a sensation in America by predicting Christ would return October 22, 1844. On October 28, 1992, believers from hundreds of churches in Seoul, South Korea, stood in the streets awaiting the end of the world. Many had abandoned school, job and family in anticipation of "the Rapture."[1]

In each case, the moment passed and history marched on. Whatever impact the disappointment may have had on the faith of individual believers, this record of fizzled predictions has produced serious and unfortunate consequences on a larger scale.

First, it has conveyed to others a wanton disregard for Jesus' assurance that "of that day and hour no one knows, not even the angels of heaven, but My Father only" (Matthew 24:36). Even nonbelievers can detect in these prognostications a prideful arrogance which refuses to accept that "it is not for you to know times or seasons which the Father has put in His own authority" (Acts 1:7).

Second, it has served to bolster the smug attitude of those who derisively ask, "Where is the promise of His coming? For since the fathers fell asleep, all things continue as they were from the beginning of creation" (2 Peter 3:4). After a while, the boy who cries wolf is laughed at or ignored.

Third, it has fostered even among well-meaning Christians the notion that Christ's Return is a random event. Although the previous guesses were obviously wrong, many believe that in "God's lottery in the sky," the Second Coming "number" could still come up at any time. All this reveals a baffling ignorance of traditional Christian teachings which indicate a clear chain of events to be fulfilled during the last days.

A proper understanding of the end times cannot be based on mere human speculation—however sincere, well-intentioned, or even "biblically grounded." It must originate from the sacred Tradition of the Holy Catholic and Apostolic Church, which treats this subject clearly and thoroughly.

The primary articulators of this Tradition are the Apostles and Fathers of the Church. Many modern thinkers, in their love of "originality" and their disdain for authority, consensus, and wisdom, dismiss such sources of knowledge. But in so doing, they leave themselves benighted in a darkness of their own choosing. Christians can afford no such stupidity.

The Fathers speak from a perspective of far greater spiritual clarity than is generally accessible today. The holiness of their lives and the affirmative testimony of the ensuing centuries give their words a weight no modern teacher's can claim. It is Holy Tradition, transmitted through the Fathers, which gives Christians a firm basis for understanding and critiquing the events which surround them.

Does it Really Matter?

Because of varied opinions surrounding the last days, many Christians prefer to avoid the subject altogether, deeming it too difficult to understand, and in any case, irrelevant to the salvation of their souls. Even if they suspect, based on the evils which abound in the contemporary world, that conditions may indeed be ripe for the end times, they do nothing about it.

But while Christ is "the same yesterday, today, and forever" (Hebrews 13:8), the last Christians must nevertheless labor more tomorrow than they did yesterday in order not to be overwhelmed by the spirit of this age. "They are wrong," admonished Father Seraphim Rose, "who teach that, because the end of the world is at hand, we must sit still, make no great efforts, simply preserve the doctrine that has been handed down to us, and hand it back, like the buried talent of the worthless servant (Matt. 25:24-30), to the Lord at His Coming! . . . Let us then struggle while it is still day, with the time and the weapons which our All-merciful God has given us!"[2]

Are the end times irrelevant? There is scarcely a subject in Christian literature which has been treated more exhaustively. References to Christ's Return and Judgment permeate the Bible, especially the New Testament. The Holy Fathers wrote extensive commentaries on the last days, and the petition of Saint Basil the Great figures prominently in prayer books: "Grant us to pass the night of the whole present life with wakeful heart and sober thought, ever expecting the coming of the radiant day of the appearing of Thy only-begotten Son, our Lord and God and Saviour, Jesus Christ, when the Judge of all will come with glory to render to each according to their deeds."[3]

The Scriptures and the Holy Fathers emphasize that

Christians should never forget their Lord will return—daily activity should focus on this ultimate reality. "Cease not to inquire of thy Mother the Church: when the hoped-for Bridegroom shall come," counseled Saint Ephraim the Syrian in the fourth century. "Ask about, and ascertain the signs of His coming, for the Judge will not tarry. Cease not to ask, though thou shalt not know with accuracy; cease not to flee to the aid of them that know of this exactly."[4]

Worldly Antagonism

Christians can be intimidated into avoiding the subject of the end times simply because modern society discourages it. The prospect of this world "ending," after all, renders all worldly pursuits meaningless. Most contemporary attitudes are based on a utopian, rather than Christian, viewpoint (even when this is not admitted or even consciously recognized). The world may not be perfect at present, says much of society, but it is perfectible. And someday—with man as the measure of all things—brotherly love and peace will be realized on this earth. "Thus, everything is fine!" contemporary Orthodox theologian Archbishop Averky mimics sarcastically. "It is not necessary to labor over oneself, and no spiritual struggle is required; the fasts may be abolished. Everything will get better *all by itself*, until the Kingdom of God is finally established on earth with universal earthly satisfaction and blessedness."[5]

Even Christians, to the degree that secular thinking has invaded their understanding, may bypass the harsher aspects of the end times and take refuge in comforting but fallacious concepts such as chiliasm (belief in a literal thousand-year reign of Christ which is yet to come) or the rapture (the taking up of Christians into heaven before the Great Tribulation).

The desire of modern men, whether secular or "Christian," for a specifically non-Christian history devoid of any end times is well documented—and completely understandable. Even popular musicians, usually innocent of depth of thought, sing of "coming together" and "giving peace a chance." In every arena of contemporary human enterprise—economic, political, religious or social—the message of "making a better world for man" is trumpeted.

"Theoretically perhaps," admonished Archbishop Averky, "... we admit the end of the world, the Second Coming of Christ, the Last Judgment, and the future life, but in practice we live and act as if none of this is to be expected and we have only to make ourselves comfortable here on earth by providing for ourselves all sorts of good things and conveniences."[6]

Ignorance or defiance of truth does not lessen truth's actuality, however. Christians may not shrug off the end times as an archaic, hyper-religious notion just because it is a difficult subject. The world invites them to complacency and comfort, but Jesus urges vigilance: "Watch therefore, and pray always that you may be counted worthy to escape all these things that will come to pass" (Luke 21:36).

Signs of the Times

Fortunately, God has ordained a series of milestones to alert his besieged children to crucial historical events. The Lord showed that such indicators may be ignored only at one's peril, and He reserved a heaping measure of indignation for those who neither observe nor understand these signals: "Hypocrites! You know how to discern the face of the sky, but you cannot discern the signs of the times" (Matthew 16:3).

Signs are not given so the idle or curious can predict dates and speculate on personalities, but so believers can prepare to do battle against evil. Although the Lord called His generation "wicked and adulterous" (Matthew 16:4) for seeking a sign, in His mercy and compassion he allowed that specific things would occur during the last days to warn spiritually weakened mankind. "So you also, when you see all these things, know that it is near—at the doors! Assuredly, I say to you, this generation will by no means pass away till all these things take place" (Matthew 24:33, 34).

If a driver purposefully ignores a "Bridge Out" sign and sinks his car in the river, he may justifiably be considered idiotic. By the same token, those who ignore the divine signs which have been established to warn mankind voluntarily place themselves at the greatest possible risk. "Signs do occur in history from time to time," affirmed Roman Catholic author Vincent Miceli, "not to fix the day, but to remind us that the Antichrist and the final struggle between the Church and her enemies is daily approaching."[7]

What signs are Christians to watch for thus? The recently canonized Saint Ignatius Brianchaninov, a nineteenth-century Russian bishop, insisted that the corrupt state of men's souls and of society will itself be a divine warning: "Universal debauchery, together with the most abundant material progress which engendered it, will be the sign of the end of the age and the approaching terrible judgment of Christ."[8]

However, the signs which God has ordained for the end times are far more detailed and specific even than this. Blessed Augustine, one of the great Western Fathers of the fourth and fifth centuries, orders the major ones as follows: "In connection with [the last] judgment the following events shall come to pass, as we have learned: Elias the Tishbite shall come; the Jews shall believe; Antichrist shall persecute; Christ shall judge; the dead shall rise; the good and the wicked shall be separated; the world shall be burned and renewed. All these things, we believe, shall come to pass; but how, or in what order, human understanding cannot perfectly teach us, but only the experience of the events themselves. My opinion, however, is, that they will happen in the order in which I have related them."[9]

[1] *The Atlanta Journal,* Oct. 28, 1992, p. A13.

[2] Christensen, *Not of This World,* p. 633.

[3] *Prayer Book,* Holy Trinity Monastery, p. 16.

[4] *Works of the Venerable Ephraim the Syrian,* Moscow, 1850, Vol. IV, p. 133, as quoted in Molchanoff, *Antichrist,* p. 27.

[5] *The Apocalypse of St. John,* p. 228.

[6] *Stand Fast in the Truth,* pp. 10-11.

[7] *The Antichrist*, p. 122.

[8] "On the Kingdom of God," *Epiphany Journal*, Vol. 9, No. 1, Fall 1988, p. 55.

[9] *The City of God*, Book XX, ch. 30, p. 762.

Chapter 3

The Great World Empires

Civilizations have been destroyed, many of them.
But never mankind. But this time it is different.
—*Joseph Weizenbaum*

One night sometime during the fifth century B.C., Nebuchadnezzar "had dreams; and his spirit was so troubled that his sleep left him" (Daniel 2:1). Since he was the king of Babylon, if he had a bad night, everyone else did too. Nebuchadnezzar got up in the dark and summoned his magicians, astrologers and sorcerers. He commanded them to interpret his dream.

"Certainly," the king's wise men responded. "Just tell us your dream and we'll interpret it."

Nebuchadnezzar must have been feeling a little cagey, for he insisted not only that they interpret his dream, but that they first tell *him* what it was! The penalty for failure was to be cut in pieces. Predictably, the magicians and astrologers were stymied and agitated at the royal request. They would certainly have met an early demise, had it not been for Daniel.

Daniel, a Jew in captivity, heard what was happening

and started to pray, knowing that only God could inspire him to meet the king's demand. Then he went to Nebuchadnezzar and said, "There is a God in heaven who reveals secrets, and He has made known . . . what will be in the latter days" (Daniel 2:28). Daniel understood that, although the king's dream dealt with the entire scope of sacred history, its purpose was to shed light on the "latter" or last days.

Having gained Nebuchadnezzar's ear, Daniel proceeded to reveal and interpret his dream: "You, O king, were watching; and behold, a great image! This great image, whose splendor was excellent, stood before you; and its form was awesome. This image's head was of fine gold, its chest and arms of silver, its belly and thighs of bronze, its legs of iron, its feet partly of iron and partly of clay. You watched while a stone was cut out without hands, which struck the image on its feet of iron and clay, and broke them in pieces. . . .

"You, O King . . . are this head of gold. But after you shall arise another kingdom inferior to yours; then another, a third kingdom of bronze, which shall rule over all the earth. And the fourth kingdom shall be as strong as iron, inasmuch as iron breaks in pieces and shatters everything. . . . Whereas you saw the feet and toes, partly of potter's clay and partly of iron, the kingdom shall be divided. . . . And as the toes of the feet were partly of iron and partly of clay, so the kingdom shall be partly strong and partly fragile. . . . And in the days of these kings the God of heaven will set up a kingdom which shall never be destroyed; and the kingdom shall not be left to other people; it shall break in pieces and consume all these kingdoms, and it shall stand forever" (Daniel 2:31-44).

The Four Metals

There is quite broad agreement among the Holy Fathers and modern scholars that the four kingdoms of Nebuchadnezzar's dream refer to specific earthly empires. Saint Cyril of Jerusalem explained that "as the first kingdom [gold] which became renowned was that of the Assyrians, and the second [silver], that of the Medes and Persians together, and after these, that of the Macedonians was the third [bronze], so the fourth kingdom [iron] now is that of the Romans."[1]

The Roman kingdom had two distinct periods, represented by the legs and the feet. The legs of the first period are wholly of iron and thus very strong. Yet there are two legs, suggesting the historical division of the Roman Empire into East and West. The feet, representing the second Roman period, are partly of iron and partly of clay. Because of this mixing, they are weaker. The ten toes suggest the ten nations (called "ten horns" in Daniel 7:7) of the final phase of the Roman Empire from which Antichrist is to make his appearance. This phase, as we will see, is our modern times.

Second-century Bishop Saint Irenaeus noted the great division of humanity which the ten toes of the figure represent: "For that the kingdom must be divided, and thus come to ruin, the Lord [declares when He] says: 'Every kingdom divided against itself . . . shall not stand.' It must be, therefore, that the kingdom, the city, and the house be divided into ten; and for this reason He has already foreshadowed the partition and division [which shall take place]. . . . The ten toes, therefore, are these ten kings, among whom the kingdom shall be partitioned, of whom some indeed shall be strong and active, or energetic; others, again, shall be sluggish and useless, and shall not agree; as also Daniel says: 'Some part of the kingdom shall be strong, and part shall be broken from it. As thou sawest the iron mixed with the baked clay, there shall be minglings among the human race, but no cohesion one with the other, just as iron cannot be welded on to pottery ware.' "[2]

The terrible image in the king's dream is a composite of metals, from soft yet precious gold to hard yet common iron. Protestant commentator C.I. Scofield suggested that these world empires reflect a gradual decrease in spiritual refinement and a corresponding increase in material strength over the course of history: "From the head of gold (v. 38) to the iron of the fourth kingdom (Rome) there is deterioration in fineness, but increase of strength (v. 40). Then comes the deterioration of the fourth kingdom in that very quality— strength. . . . The kingdom is divided into two, the legs (eastern and western empires), and these are again divided into kingdoms, the number of which, when the Stone smites the image, will be ten (toes)."[3]

This view of history has in fact been widely held. "The ancients," wrote Thomas Molnar, ". . . as witness Ovid's *Metamorphoses,* believed that a Golden Age preceded the Silver Age, and that they themselves lived in an Iron Age."[4] But in what sense were the pagan kingdoms preceding the birth of Christ actually better than the Roman Empire, in which Jesus actually became incarnate?

The Babylonians worshiped the sun god, Shamash, while the Persians worshiped their god of light, Ahura-Mazdah. The Greeks worshiped a pantheon of gods residing in Mt. Olympus. Romans worshiped the Greek gods also, but renamed them (e.g., Jupiter instead of Zeus). While the men of these ancient kingdoms were pagan, most at least believed in higher, spiritual powers. "It is true that the pre-modern societies were ignorant of the real identity of the giver of life," wrote contemporary writer Father Michael Oleksa, "but their basic intuition that there is a sacred (rather than a natural power as in the modern attitude) behind the cosmos was essentially valid from a Christian viewpoint."[5]

Though ignorant of the true nature of the objects of their devotion, these men tended to be devout. For example, Saint Paul observed that the Greek Athenians worshiped at the shrine of "the Unknown God" (see Acts 17:22, 23). He used their devotion to this deity to instruct them concerning the true God of all creation.

When God chose to reveal Himself fully, He selected a certain race, the Jews, to be the initial recipients of His Self-revelation. He taught them through prophets and called them His "chosen people." Although the Jews often disobeyed their God (and paid a heavy penalty for it!), they never rejected a spiritual world-view. They slipped into idolatry, but not atheism.

However far from God's truth men may have been during those ancient times, few would have denied that there *was* a truth. The concept of atheism was so repugnant and foreign that early Christians were sometimes ignorantly accused of this very thing! Contemporary writer Father Michael Azkoul relates that "Saint Polycarp of Smyrna was martyred by a pagan mob for 'atheism,' that is, for denying 'the gods of the city' in the name of Christ *(Martyr. Poly.* 3.3)."[6]

This point was vividly illustrated by Marcus Aurelius, who at first raged against Christians. Amazed by the power of their prayers on his behalf, the emperor finally admitted to the Roman Senate that "those whom we suppose to be atheists, have God as their ruling power entrenched in their conscience."[7]

The Greeks and Romans were predominantly polytheists. Yet the Greco-Roman civilization ultimately gave birth to what might be called theoretical atheism, or the conscious denial of deity. Socrates was condemned by the Athenians for atheism, because he did not believe in the city's goddess, Athena. Cicero claimed the existence of gods could not be proved, and Lucretius asserted that the cosmos was solely material.

With the rise of the fourth kingdom (Rome), man began to define the cosmos solely in terms of himself. He refused, as Father Seraphim Rose put it, "to acknowledge any arbiter of fact save the proud human reason."[8] He venerated, if not worshiped, his rational mind, and expected it to unravel all the knots in the universe.

Mankind claimed no longer to need God. Under these conditions, atheism (and its corollary, nihilism) became the province not only of philosophers, but of the common man. Consequently, the Romans (meaning all under the dominion and influence of this kingdom—even up to the present times) became both stronger in a material sense and far more crude spiritually.

The Four Beasts

Daniel also described the four kingdoms as predatory animals: "And four great beasts came up from the sea, each different from the other. The first was like a lion, and had eagle's wings. I watched till its wings were plucked off; and it was lifted up from the earth and made to stand on two feet like a man, and a man's heart was given to it.

"And suddenly another beast, a second, like a bear. It was raised up on one side, and had three ribs in its mouth between its teeth. And they said thus to it: 'Arise, devour much flesh!' After this I looked, and there was another, like a leopard, which had on its back four wings of a bird. The beast also had four heads, and dominion was given to it.

"After this I saw in the night visions, and behold, a fourth beast, dreadful and terrible, exceedingly strong. It had huge iron teeth; it was devouring, breaking in pieces, and trampling the residue with its feet. It was different from all the beasts that were before it, and it had ten horns.

"I was considering the horns, and there was another horn, a little one, coming up among them, before whom three of the first horns were plucked out by the roots [Rome: final form of fourth world empire]. And there, in this horn, were eyes like the eyes of a man, and a mouth speaking pompous words" (Daniel 7:3-8).

Again, there is general agreement as to the world empires which these beasts represent. The first is considered to be Babylon, the second Medo-Persia, the third Greece and the fourth Rome. In Daniel's vision it is the fourth beast which represents the condition of the world when the grim events of the end times are to unfold. This beast is much different from the preceding ones. It is indomitable and ruthless, without self-restraint. The fourth beast, like the fourth kingdom, describes a world that has rejected God and truth.

In this milieu a leader is to come forth who will combine all the worst traits of this fallen humanity. So unnerving, so profoundly abnormal was the vision of this society and its leader that Daniel begged God for clarification: "Then I wished to know the truth about the fourth beast, which was different from all the others, exceedingly dreadful . . . and the ten horns that were on its head, and the other horn which came up, before which three fell, namely, that horn which had eyes and a mouth which spoke pompous words, whose appearance was greater than his fellows.

"I was watching; and the same horn was making war against the saints, and prevailing against them, until the Ancient of Days came, and . . . he said: 'The fourth beast shall be a fourth kingdom on earth, which shall be different from all other kingdoms, and shall devour the whole earth, trample it and break it in pieces. The ten horns are ten kings who shall arise from this kingdom. And another shall rise after them; he shall be different from the first ones, and shall subdue three kings' " (Daniel 7:19-24).

Saint Hippolytus (d. 236) declares the "little horn" of Daniel's vision to be Antichrist: "And amid these another little horn shall rise, which is that of Antichrist."[9] He will be a deceptive leader who will at first appear meek, then ruthlessly extinguish his enemies until he overpowers the entire world. Antichrist is thus predicted to reign at the end of the Roman kingdom. Saint Cyril of Jerusalem wrote that the "Antichrist is to come when the times of the Roman empire shall have been fulfilled, and the end of the world is now drawing near."[10]

But how can this be understood in modern terms, since the Roman Empire apparently "fell" centuries ago? Bernard McGinn pointed out that Christians have traditionally believed Rome would last until the end times: "Since Rome had come to be identified with the last of the four world empires symbolized by the statue of the second chapter of Daniel, her empire was meant to endure down to the end of the world."[11]

Rome *has* in fact lasted until the end times. To see this, however, one must understand how the Roman Empire was transformed over the course of history. In the fourth century Emperor Constantine the Great moved his capital to Byzantium, naming it the second "Rome." When Constantinople fell to the Turks in the fifteenth century, Orthodox Christian Moscow became the third "Rome." But even more important than these geographical changes was the transformation of the "Roman Empire" from a merely political/administrative entity into a spiritual monarchy.

Archimandrite Panteleimon of Holy Trinity Monastery in Jordanville, New York, explained this as follows: "The Roman Empire [means] imperial (monarchial) power in general. Concerning such power we should understand it to be a monarchy which has the ability to control social movement, and at the same time adhere to Christian principles. . . . Since the Antichrist will have as his main task the goal of attracting the people away from Christ, he therefore will not arrive if monarchy is still in control."[12]

The Ten Horns

The image of a beast with ten horns appears also in the New Testament. Saint John the Theologian records this vision: "Then I stood on the sand of the sea. And I saw a beast rising up out of the sea, having seven heads and ten horns, and on his horns ten crowns, and on his heads a blasphemous name. Now the beast which I saw was like a leopard, his feet were like the feet of a bear, and his mouth like the mouth of a lion. The dragon gave him his power, his throne, and great authority" (Revelation 13:1, 2).

Saint John reveals that the most powerful king of

the most powerful kingdom in history will have perhaps the shortest reign, figuratively referred to as one hour: "The ten horns which you saw are ten kings who have received no kingdom as yet, but they receive authority for one hour as kings with the beast. These are of one mind, and they will give their power and authority to the beast" (Revelation 17:12, 13).

The beast is to receive his earthly support from these ten kingdoms, which will be of "one mind" with him. "And the ten horns which you saw on the beast, these will hate the harlot, make her desolate and naked, eat her flesh and burn her with fire. For God has put it into their hearts to fulfill His purpose, to be of one mind, and to give their kingdom to the beast, until the words of God are fulfilled" (Revelation 17:16, 17).

This vision offers another view of the anti-hero of the end times. "This beast is the Antichrist," declared Archbishop Averky unequivocally. "He is 'of the seven,' because he has made his appearance from one of these kingdoms."[13]

The ten horns refer to ten kingdoms of the ancient Roman Empire which will unite to give Antichrist his political base. Seven will support him willingly, but three will require "persuasion." According to Saint Cyril of Jerusalem, "There shall rise up together ten kings of the Romans, reigning in different parts perhaps, but all about the same time; and after these an eleventh, the Antichrist, who by his magical craft shall seize upon the Roman power; and of the kings who reigned before him, *three he shall humble,* and the remaining seven he shall keep in subjection to himself."[14]

Lactantius, a fourth-century scholar, Christian apologist, and tutor to the son of Emperor Constantine, prophesied that Antichrist would come to power by means of warfare and conquest: "A sword will travel through the world cutting down everything and laying all things low like a harvested crop. The cause of this devastation and confusion will be the fact that the Roman name, which now rules the world, will be taken from the earth [see Chapter 6]. . . . There will be no end of deadly wars until ten kings will emerge simultaneously. They will divide the world to destroy and not to govern it. . . .

"Then a mighty enemy from the far North will suddenly rise up against them. When he has destroyed the three who control Asia he will be taken into alliance with the others and will be made their chief. He will afflict the world with unbearable tyranny . . . and will work for things abominable and accursed."[15]

Contemporary writer Archpriest Boris Molchanoff offered this wartime scenario: "It is entirely possible that [Antichrist] will begin his activity during a world war, when nations, enduring all the horrors thereof, will envision no other escape from a calamitous deadlock, for all the hidden levers for the resolution of the war will be in the hands of a secret society assisting the Antichrist. Antichrist will set forth a plan for the resolution of the world-wide crisis which will be most felicitous from the point of view of political and social wisdom—the establishment of a unified political and social order on a universal scale. Exhausted from the shock of war, spiritually blind humanity will not only fail to perceive this scheme as an insidious trap for itself, designed to lure it into inescapable and merciless bondage, but, on the contrary, will acknowledge it as a work of scholarship and genius."[16]

Although Antichrist will be a man, he is described in Saint John's vision as arising from the sea, and receiving power from a dragon. The sea is understood to represent mankind, and the dragon clearly refers to Satan. "Almost all interpreters understand [that Antichrist] . . . comes out of the 'sea of life,' that is in the midst of the human race which is agitated like a sea," wrote Archbishop Averky. ". . . He will not be an incarnate devil as some have thought, but a man. . . . This authority he will receive with the help of the dragon or the devil."[17]

The Seven Kings

The world's great empires are also described in terms of consecutive kings. The last of these is to be the Antichrist, whose reign will be brief, lasting only "a short time." That he will come to power is certain, and also certain is his defeat, for the Apostle states that he will go "to perdition": "There are also seven kings. Five have fallen, one is, and the other has not yet come. And when he comes, he must continue a short time. The beast that was, and is not, is himself also the eighth, and is of the seven, and is going to perdition" (Revelation 17:10, 11).

Saint Andrew of Caesarea, underscoring the thinking of yet another Father, wrote in the fifth century that "under the name of five kings who have fallen out of the seven, Blessed Hippolytus understands ages, of which five are already passed. The sixth, in which the Apostle saw this, is still going on, and the seventh age which follows upon the sixth has not yet come, but when it comes it will not continue long . . . or (the kings) are the seven kingdoms which have been from the beginning of the world until now; five have already fallen, the sixth—under which the revelation was made—was ancient Rome, and the seventh is yet to come—this is the New Rome."

Prophecy Fulfilled

It is provocative to examine history and contemporary events in search of the fulfillment of these colossal prophecies. They are given, after all, for instruction and admonition, lest "that Day come on you unexpectedly" (Luke 21:34). Yet Christians should remember that Satan also knows the Scriptures! He tempted Christ with them, saying, "It is written: 'He shall give His angels charge over you' " (Matthew 4:6).

As Shakespeare pointed out, "The devil can cite Scripture for his purpose."[18] The evil one is well aware of all that the Bible has to say about him and, as he is more subtle and clever than the mind of man can fathom, he will almost certainly fulfill scriptural prophecies in some unexpected way. Christians must guard against assigning interpretations based on fallen human reason, or confidently assuming that "Y" is impossible because "X" has not happened yet.

Blessed Augustine worried that those watching for the signs of the times would be taken in just as surely as others who paid no attention to them. "As for the ten kings," Augustine wrote, "whom, as it seems, Antichrist is to find in the person of ten individuals when he comes, I own I am afraid we may be deceived in this, and that he may come unexpectedly while there are not ten kings living in the Roman world."[19]

[1] "Catechetical Lectures," Lecture XV, part 13, in *Nicene and Post-Nicene Fathers*, Vol. VII, p. 108.

[2] "Against Heresies," Book V, ch. XXVI, in *The Ante-Nicene Fathers*, Vol. I, p. 555.

[3] C.I. Scofield, ed., *Holy Bible*, Oxford University Press, p. 899.

[4] *Utopia: The Perennial Heresy*, p. 16.

[5] "Icons and the Cosmos," *Epiphany Journal*, Vol. 8, No. 4, Summer 1988, p. 71.

[6] *Anti-Christianity: The New Atheism*, p. 4.

[7] "First Apology of Justin Marytr," in *The Ante-Nicene Fathers*, Vol. I, p. 187.

[8] *Nihilism*, p. 18.

[9] Fragments from commentaries, in *The Ante-Nicene Fathers*, Vol. V, p. 190.

[10] "Catechetical Lectures," Lecture XV, part 12, in *Nicene and Post-Nicene Fathers*, Vol. VII, p. 107.

[11] *Apocalyptic Spirituality*, p. 84.

[12] *A Ray of Light*, p. 38.

[13] *The Apocalypse of St. John*, p. 177.

[14] "Catechetical Lectures," *loc. cit.*

[15] "The Blessed Life," Book VII of *Divine Institutes*, from *Apocalyptic Spirituality*, pp. 59-60.

[16] *Antichrist,* p. 4.
[17] *The Apocalypse of St. John,* p. 143.
[18] *The Merchant of Venice,* Act I, scene iii, line 99.
[19] *The City of God,* Book XX, ch. 23, p. 748.

Chapter 4

The Preparation of Israel

*And so it will be to the end of the world, even
when gods disappear from the earth; they will
fall down before idols just the same.*
—*Fyodor Dostoevsky*

One of the great ironies of the Old Testament is that
an entire nation was enslaved as a result of one of its
children being sold into slavery. The story of Joseph
(Genesis 30—50) is an astonishing revelation of the
way God works in human hearts and in sacred history.
In addition, it offers important insights about the end
times.

Joseph, the beloved son of his father Jacob, was sold
into slavery by his jealous brothers. Joseph was taken to
Egypt, where his diligence and loyalty were in time
rewarded. He was appointed governor over the land,
and because of his careful storing of grain during seven
years of plenty, he could disburse these reserves to the
people during the following seven years of drought.

Joseph's brothers came to Egypt during the drought
to buy grain. He tested them to see if they had repented

of their evil against him. When he saw that they had, Joseph was reconciled to his brothers, and the entire household of Jacob relocated to Egypt.

In time the Israelites became a great multitude and were enslaved by the Egyptians. God then sent Moses to challenge Pharaoh with miraculous signs, plagues, and finally destruction. God thus freed His people from slavery and led them to the Promised Land through the Red Sea. When Pharaoh tried to follow, the walls of the sea, which had been held back allowing Israel to walk on dry land, suddenly crashed down, destroying his army.

Lactantius considered the story of Joseph to be a metaphor for the last days. (Although he does not mention it, the seven years of drought may symbolize the seven years of Antichrist's reign.) "Though so famous and wonderful a deed shows God's power to men in the present, it was also the presignification and figure of something greater that God is to do in the final consummation of the ages—he will free his people from the slavery of the world. Then, because there was one people of God who dwelt in the midst of one nation, Egypt alone was struck; now, because the people of God are gathered from all languages and dwell among all nations and are oppressed by their rule, all nations, that is, the whole world, must be struck by divine blows, so that God's just and devout people may be freed. Just as then signs were given that showed the coming slaughter to the Egyptians, so at the end there will be fearful prodigies in all the world's elements by which all nations will grasp the imminent destruction."[1]

In a sense, Israel represents the wall upon which God's "handwriting" appears (Daniel 5). The world has come to know its Creator largely because of the Jews. Whether this ancient, "chosen" people obeyed the Lord or defied Him, they have nevertheless served as examples and warnings to all mankind. Their history is a guidebook to what should, shouldn't, and will yet be done.

The *Lenten Triodion* contains the following prayer: "O Lord, the Jews condemned Thee to death, who art the Life of all; with Moses' rod Thou hast led them on dry ground through the Red Sea, yet they nailed Thee to the Cross. . . . See how the lawless synagogue has condemned to death the King of the Creation! They were not ashamed when He recalled His blessings, saying: 'O My people, what have I done unto you? Have I not filled Judaea with miracles? Have I not raised the dead by My word alone? Have I not healed every sickness and disease? How then have ye repaid Me? Why have ye forgotten Me? In return for healing, ye have given Me blows; in return for life, ye are putting Me to death. Ye hang upon the Cross your Benefactor as an evildoer, your Lawgiver as a transgressor of the Law, the King of all as one condemned.' "[2]

In failing to recognize their Messiah, the Jews confirmed their blindness. In crucifying Him, they assured their destruction. Israel condemned the Temple of God (Christ's Body), and in consequence God condemned the temple of Israel. This is exactly what Jesus told His disciples would happen before either event took place: "And His disciples came up to show Him the buildings of the temple. And Jesus said to them, 'Do you not see all these things? Assuredly, I say to you, not one stone shall be left here upon another, that shall not be thrown down' " (Matthew 24:1, 2).

Having led their own King to death on the Cross, the Jews shunned their Protector, and they would consequently be taken captive, dispersed, and killed. "For these are the days of vengeance, that all things which are written may be fulfilled. . . . And they will fall by the edge of the sword, and be led away captive into all nations. And Jerusalem will be trampled by Gentiles until the times of the Gentiles are fulfilled" (Luke 21:22, 24).

Obedient (though unknowingly) to God's will, the Roman Emperor Titus destroyed Jerusalem in A.D. 70, slaughtering thousands of Jews and sending the rest into exile. Herod's magnificent temple, completed just years earlier, was decimated. As Jesus had foretold, there was literally not one stone left upon another. The destruction was so complete that even sophisticated, high-tech archeologists admit the exact location of the temple on the temple mount is now uncertain.

The destruction of the holy city was a fore-image of the ultimate fate which awaits the world in consequence of its rejection of Christ. We read in *Apostasy and Antichrist,* "The fall of Jerusalem was symbolic of the end of the world, but terrible though it was, it was only a pale shadow of what is to come upon mankind at the very end."[3]

For nearly two millennia the Jewish people had no permanent home, as the diaspora spread throughout the world. God had revealed, however, that Israel's punishment would eventually have an end and the Jews would be drawn back to the Promised Land. "After many days you will be visited," wrote Ezekiel. "In the latter years you will come into the land of those brought back from the sword and gathered from many people on the mountains of Israel, which had long been desolate; they were brought out of the nations, and now all of them dwell safely" (Ezekiel 38:8).

Returning Home

In 1948 the tiny state of Israel was reborn in spite of overwhelming (yet understandable) Arab hostili-ties, thus fulfilling God's prophecy to restore the Jewish homeland. The ending of Jacob's captivity meant that God's other prophecies could be fulfilled—the regathering of "the whole house of Israel."

"Therefore thus says the Lord GOD: 'Now I will bring back the captives of Jacob, and have mercy on the whole house of Israel; and I will be jealous for My holy name. . . . When I have brought them back from the peoples and gathered them out of their enemies' lands, and I am hallowed in them in the sight of many nations' " (Ezekiel 39:25, 27).

Jeremiah refers to "the north country," which could

well mean Russia and Eastern Europe, whence many Ashkenazim Jews have come back to Israel: "Behold, I will bring them from the north country, and gather them from the ends of the earth, among them the blind and the lame, the woman with child and the one who labors with child, together; a great throng shall return there" (Jeremiah 31:8).

The Lord spread them out on the earth, and the Lord will call them to return, said Zechariah: " 'Up, up! Flee from the land of the north,' says the LORD; 'for I have spread you abroad like the four winds of heaven,' says the LORD" (Zechariah 2:6).

According to the Scriptures, the flight from the North is as significant an event as Israel's deliverance from Egypt's bondage under Moses' leadership. The similarity is obvious, for in both cases the Jews were led to the Promised Land. " 'Therefore behold, the days are coming,' says the LORD, 'that it shall no more be said, "The LORD lives who brought up the children of Israel from the land of Egypt," but, "The LORD lives who brought up the children of Israel from the land of the north and from all the lands where He had driven them." For I will bring them back into their land which I gave to their fathers' " (Jeremiah 16:14, 15).

Ezekiel also confirmed this prophecy, showing that the return of the Jews to their homeland was to be a clearly defined event orchestrated by God: "Thus says the Lord GOD: 'Surely I will take the children of Israel from among the nations, wherever they have gone, and will gather them from every side and bring them into their own land' " (Ezekiel 37:21).

The Last Jewish Temple

The Prophets of old knew that the return of the children of Israel to the Promised Land would spark a deep religious revival: "For the children of Israel shall abide many days without king or prince, without sacrifice or sacred pillar, without ephod or teraphim. Afterward the children of Israel shall return and seek the LORD their God and David their king. They shall fear the LORD and His goodness in the latter days" (Hosea 3:4, 5).

Even though the temple had been destroyed, God's promise through Ezekiel remained: to "set My sanctuary in their midst forevermore. My tabernacle also shall be with them; indeed I will be their God, and they shall be My people" (Ezekiel 37:26, 27).

Micah made it clear when God's temple would be re-established: "Now it shall come to pass in the latter days that the mountain of the LORD's house shall be established on the top of the mountains, and shall be exalted above the hills; and peoples shall flow to it" (Micah 4:1). The temple will again be restored "in the latter days."

Amos also timed this historic event with his phrase "on that day," indicating the day of the Lord, or Christ's Return. The ruins are to be raised up and the temple built again "as in the days of old": "On that day I will raise up the tabernacle of David, which has fallen down, and repair its damages; I will raise up its ruins, and rebuild it as in the days of old" (Amos 9:11).

In 1981, Father Seraphim Rose gave a lecture at the University of California at Santa Cruz, in which he said, "Another sign that the times of the end are approaching is the present state of the Jews in Israel, in the city of Jerusalem. According to the prophecies of the Scriptures and the Holy Fathers, Jerusalem will be the world capital of Antichrist, and there he will rebuild the temple of Solomon where he will be worshipped as God. . . .

"Of course, it is very significant that only since 1948 has Jerusalem been once more in the hands of the Jews, and only since 1967 has the place where the temple was, the Mosque of Omar, been in their hands, since this had been in the part held by the Moslems. . . .

"If you were to ask anyone who's aware at all of political events in the world a question, 'What would be the ideal city to have as the world capital if there was going to be a world empire?'—it's obvious what the answer would be in most people's minds. It can't be New York because that's the capital of capitalism; it can't be Moscow because that's the center of Communism. It can't even be Rome, because Roman Catholicism is still some kind of limited division. The logical place is Jerusalem, because there three religions come together, three continents come together. It's the most logical place where there could be peace, brotherhood, harmony: all those things which look good, but unless they have a solid Christian foundation are not God-pleasing. These things will be used by Antichrist."[4]

Significant preparations are presently underway in Israel to restore the actual worship ceremonies formerly conducted within Solomon's temple. Sacred vessels have been formed, priestly garments sewn. As Ice and Price report in their 1992 book, *Ready to Rebuild,* "The Temple Institute, then, is preparing vessels and garments for the Temple service, and seeking to produce a valid red heifer in Israel for the future purification of the priests and worshipers in the Temple. The leaders of this organization firmly believe that we are in the *achari ha-yamim* ('last days') which include the coming of the Messiah. They expect the building of the Temple to begin shortly."[5]

The Messiah whom the Jews anticipate, however, bears little resemblance to the Jesus Christ who voluntarily died to save sinners. They look for a world leader to rule all the nations from his capital of Jerusalem, to initiate a political regime of "peace" and "prosperity," and to vindicate Israel for her centuries of suffering at Gentile hands.

"They do not want Christ as He is," cries contemporary writer Alexander Kalomiros. "They do not want the Christ Who refused to submit to the devil's temptations in the desert. . . . They want a Christ Who desires the kingdoms of the earth, a Christ Who will turn the stones into bread so that men may be satiated, a Christ who will overwhelm the world with miracles that inspire awe and constrain men to submit . . . a Christ Who will talk about this life and not the other, a Christ

Who will offer the pleasures of this life and not of the next. . . . They do not want Him as ruler of the future age, but of the present one."[6]

In a word, after two centuries of incredible suffering for their blindness, the Jews as a whole have not changed. Myopically, they still want what they wanted two thousand years ago. And this time, they will get it!

[1] "The Blessed Life," Book VII of *Divine Institutes,* from *Apocalyptic Spirituality,* Bernard McGinn, trans., p. 57.

[2] *The Lenten Triodion,* Mother Mary and Archimandrite Kallistos Ware, trans., pp. 603, 613.

[3] *Apostasy and Antichrist,* Deacon Lev Puhalo and Vasili Novakshonoff, trans., p. 22.

[4] Christensen, *Not of This World,* p. 887.

[5] *Ready to Rebuild,* pp. 136-137.

[6] *Against False Union,* pp. 8, 9.

Chapter 5

Satan in Bondage

Do not fear the devil. He who fears God will
overcome the devil; for him the devil is powerless.
—Saint Seraphim of Sarov

The Man leaps up boldly from the pit. Defiant, powerful, He stands upon the gates which, shattered by the force of His exit, have failed to contain Him. With a swift and decisive movement, He reaches back into the darkness from which He has emerged. Grasping the wrists of a woman and her husband who are too weak to escape, He draws them up easily, their frayed clothes streaming behind them. The Man's face is both stern and serene, as though mindful of, yet untroubled by, the horror in the pit. His eyes, gazing into the distance upon something which only He can see, ignore the hideous form yet thrashing in the black hole below Him.

Could this other awful form even be a man? Its terrible discolored head snarls, its jagged teeth gnash in fury, its stinking limbs shake with rage. Twisting and flailing like a wounded serpent, it cries out in murderous hatred against the Man who has left the pit. Its wrath is virulent, maniacal, threatening—yet impotent. For the form is bound, hand and foot. Chains lace it, cutting its flesh in the ferocity of their fastness. Against these fetters, which will not break for a millennium, it froths and howls in rabid frenzy. At last, exhausted and cursing, it strains to lift its opaque eyes upward. Above, He who has escaped shines with brilliant and otherworldly light. The dark form fastens its evil stare upon the Man's feet, and with unabated, venomous intent . . . waits.

This vivid scene confronts those who enter the ancient Church of Chora in Constantinople. The church dates back to the sixth century at least—some say the third century—and Christians who worshiped there before it was desecrated and turned into a Moslem mosque in 1511 understood that the fresco in the apse was a portrayal, an icon, of Christ's Resurrection. "Hail, most precious and life-giving Cross of the Lord," those believers might well have prayed, "for Thou drivest away the demons by the power of our Lord Jesus Christ crucified on thee, Who went down to hell and trampled on the power of the devil."[1]

Christian truths are represented in the painting: the pit is hell, which Christ has harrowed. The woman and her husband are Eve and Adam, and by implication, all their progeny, now rescued from the prospect of eternal damnation. The bound man is Satan, furious with his incarceration.

"The King of glory stretched out His right hand,"

exults the apocryphal Gospel of Nicodemus, "and took hold of our forefather Adam, and raised him. Then turning also to the rest, He said: Come all with me, as many as have died through the tree which he touched; for, behold, I again raise you all up through the tree of the cross. . . . The Saviour blessed Adam with the sign of the cross on his forehead, and did this also to the patriarchs, and prophets, and martyrs, and forefathers; and He took them, and sprang up out of Hades."[2]

The Bottomless Pit

Early believers, contemplating this depiction of Satan's predicament, would also have recalled the words of the Apostle John: "Then I saw an angel coming down from heaven, having the key to the bottomless pit and a great chain in his hand. He laid hold of the dragon, that serpent of old, who is the Devil and Satan, and bound him for a thousand years; and he cast him into the bottomless pit, and shut him up, and set a seal on him, so that he should deceive the nations no more till the thousand years were finished. But after these things he must be released for a little while" (Revelation 20:1-3).

These believers knew that Saint John's "thousand years" indicated not a precise year count, but the general time period between Christ's First and Second Comings. According to Saint Andrew of Caesarea, this "thousand years" represents the entire period from the Incarnation of Christ to the coming of Antichrist.

Saint John reiterates this time period in the following

verses, saying: "I saw the souls of those who had been beheaded for their witness to Jesus. . . . And they lived and reigned with Christ for a thousand years. But the rest of the dead did not live again until the thousand years were finished. This is the first resurrection. Blessed and holy is he who has part in the first resurrection. Over such the second death has no power, but they shall be priests of God and of Christ, and shall reign with Him a thousand years" (Revelation 20:4-6).

While some non-Orthodox have mistakenly interpreted these passages to promise believers a literal thousand-year reign with Christ after the Second Coming, the early Church Fathers declare that the first resurrection refers specifically to Christian baptism.

Father Michael Pomazansky explains, "Sacred Scripture clearly indicate[s] that the 'first resurrection' signifies spiritual rebirth into eternal life in Christ through baptism. . . . Proceeding from this by the thousand year reign one must understand the period of time from the very beginning of the kingdom of grace of the Church of Christ . . . until the end of the world."[3]

And according to Blessed Augustine, "But while the devil is bound, the saints reign with Christ during the same thousand years. . . . The Church even now is the kingdom of Christ, and the kingdom of heaven." Thus, "life" in the Church signifies spiritual life through baptism. Augustine continues, "Whosoever has not lived until the thousand years be finished, *i.e.* during this whole time in which the first resurrection is going on—whosoever has not heard the voice of the Son of

God, and passed from death to life—that man shall certainly in the second resurrection, the resurrection of the flesh, pass with his flesh into the second death."[4]

In Chora, as in many other Orthodox Christian churches, two icons dominate the viewer's senses, and establish the principal milestones of world history. The first, previously mentioned, is that of the Resurrection. The placement of this striking image at the church's visual focal point emphasizes that the Lord's Resurrection is the central, transforming event for mankind and all creation.

Yet the icon also reveals a sinister threat. Even at the moment of Christ's triumph, His cringing but unrepentant foe plots vengeance. Ancient believers were thus reminded that the dark presence beneath the Lord's feet is part of the eternal Story, of God's master plan, whose dread culmination is portrayed in the second icon—the Last Judgment.

The Last Judgment

Here, the Lord sits in majesty, presiding over an awesome scene in which the final fate of every soul is to be decided. Far below, Satan no longer writhes impotently. His bonds are gone and he controls a fearful underworld peopled with heinous creatures whose sole intent is to torture humans. With Leviathan jaws he consumes the unfortunate souls whom these devils have captured. The demonic aides labor to appease his insatiable appetite, even while he gulps three at a swallow. Satan thus devours in death those who, in a sense, tasted of him in life—those who were his, whether by conscious intent or by careless indifference to the Truth of God.

This is the Last Judgment. Between Christ and Satan, a set of scales hangs in eternity. Each human soul steps upon them, trembling. On one side, saints pray fervently; on the other, demons grimace and cackle—but God's justice is immutable. A soul weighted by unforgiven sins tips the scales and falls into the gleeful hands of the tormentors, who carry it to their master's devouring jaws. A repentant soul floats to the presence of the Blessed, while fearful Christians pray, "Snatch me from the jaws of the pernicious serpent, who is ravening to devour me and drag me down to hell alive."[5]

As the Resurrection is the defining event of the world's past, the Last Judgment is the defining event of its future. While Christ's death and burial "sowed good seed" of the Word into the "field" of the world (and ordained the toleration of both bad and good together for a season), His Return will complete the harvest, and permanently separate good from evil. As the Lord taught in His parable of the wheat and tares, "Let both grow together until the harvest, and at the time of harvest I will say to the reapers, 'First gather together the tares and bind them in bundles to burn them, but gather the wheat into my barn' " (Matthew 13:30).

The Church Age

Between these two events the greatest undertaking of all time unfolds: the drawing into Christ's Church of all those who believe and are baptized in Him. The Lord's Resurrection opened the way for *all* people (not merely the "chosen people" of the Jews) to believe in the Messiah and be saved.

As Jaroslav Pelikan points out, this view was common in the early Christian world: "Augustine set the standard for most catholic exegesis in the West . . . in favor of the view that the thousand years of that text [Revelation 20] referred to the history of the church."[6]

The Church age was made possible by putting on "restriction" him who for so long had deceived and blinded mankind. Originally, all of God's creation was created "good." When Adam sinned in disobeying God, however, he brought upon himself corruption and death. Having been duped by Satan and having obeyed the evil one instead of God, man was ordered out of Paradise and away from God's presence. Adam's fall not only brought the stain of sin to all humanity, but at the same time brought down the earthly kingdom over which he was lord.

Consequently, the nature of this world also changed; fallen creation opened itself up to become the place of Satan's house and kingdom. Recall his later boast to Jesus: "Then the devil, taking Him up on a high mountain, showed Him all the kingdoms of the world in a moment of time. And the devil said to Him, 'All this authority I will give You, and their glory; for this has been delivered to me, and I give it to whomever I wish'" (Luke 4:5, 6).

As he tempted Christ the Lord and failed, so Satan

has tempted fallen mankind throughout history to worship him in return for the temporal power and counterfeit glory he can bestow through his worldly kingdom. He has succeeded on a grand scale, for, other than God's people, first the Hebrews and then Christians, each human society has instituted some form of idol worship associated with material, this-worldly well-being. The manmade religions of earth, though some may sound attractive, are all satanic at root, for the psalmist testifies, "All the gods of the nations are demons" (Psalm 95:5, Septuagint).

In order for Christ to reach spiritually weak mankind, He had to neutralize the deceptive dictator who had captivated them. Saint John Chrysostom, the fifth-century patriarch of Constantinople, declared that the Lord was actually referring to Satan as the "strong man" when He said, "No one can enter a strong man's house and plunder his goods, unless he first binds the strong man. And then he will plunder his house" (Mark 3:27).

Christ came to a world lost in unbelief and initiated an unprecedented phase of human experience by "casting out" the "ruler of this world" and thus denying him the full exercise of his evil powers. "Now is the judgment of this world," said Jesus, as He prepared to go to the Cross. "Now the ruler of this world will be cast out" (John 12:31).

After Christ's Resurrection, Satan's influence on earth was severely diminished. No longer could he operate openly, as a strong man in control of his own house, but only secretly, mysteriously, underhandedly. For the first time since Adam and Eve, the path from man to God was restored. "Orthodox Christians who have experienced the life of grace in the Church can well understand what Protestants cannot," wrote contemporary Orthodox theologian Father Michael Pomazansky: "that the 'thousand years' (the whole period) of Christ's reign with His saints and the limited power of the devil is *now*."[7]

The Holy Spirit, operating through the Church, was given to draw people to the saving Truth of Christ. As a result, Christianity flourished even in the face of great persecution and the gospel was spread over the earth. "With the coming of the incarnate Son of God on earth," wrote Archbishop Averky, "—and in particular from the moment of His redemption of mankind through His death on the Cross—Satan was bound, paganism was cast down, and there came upon earth the thousand-year reign of Christ . . . the establishment on earth of the Church of Christ."[8]

The marriage of Christ to His Church was thus prepared, and all people, "both bad and good," as Matthew records, were invited to the feast. The Lord described this in a revealing parable:

"The kingdom of heaven is like a certain king who arranged a marriage for his son, and sent out his servants to call those who were invited to the wedding; and they were not willing to come. Again, he sent out other servants, saying, 'Tell those who are invited, "See, I have prepared my dinner; my oxen and fatted cattle are killed, and all things are ready. Come to the wedding." ' But they made light of it and went their ways, one to his own farm, another to his business. And the rest seized his servants, treated them spitefully, and killed them. But when the king heard about it, he was furious. And he sent out his armies, destroyed those murderers, and burned up their city.

"Then he said to his servants, 'The wedding is ready, but those who were invited were not worthy. Therefore go into the highways, and as many as you find, invite to the wedding.' So those servants went out into the highways and gathered together all whom they found, both bad and good. And the wedding hall was filled with guests.

"But when the king came in to see the guests, he saw a man there who did not have on a wedding garment. So he said to him, 'Friend, how did you come in here without a wedding garment?' And he was speechless. Then the king said to the servants, 'Bind him hand and foot, take him away, and cast him into outer darkness; there will be weeping and gnashing of teeth' " (Matthew 22:2-13).

It is notable that in this parable only one individual, of all those who came, received the Lord's censure for not wearing a wedding garment. Since in Jesus' culture wedding garments were provided by the host, for a guest not to wear one shows deliberate disrespect and rudeness. This strongly suggests that the intruder was Satan, and adds further confirmation that the evil one was imprisoned during the days of the Church's formation, for the king commanded his servants to "bind him hand and foot, take him away, and cast him into outer darkness"!

The Gospel Preached

With Satan thus restrained, Christianity grew steadily. By the time of the Middle Ages, European society, East and West, held a Christ-centered world-view. Missionary activity flourished, motivated by the Lord's command to "go into all the world and preach the gospel to every creature" (Mark 16:15).

Satan's period of bondage is further linked to the preaching of Christ's gospel. "And this gospel of the kingdom will be preached in all the world as a witness to all the nations, and then the end will come" (Matthew 24:14). This also has been given as another sign of the last days: the end cannot take place until all people have had a chance to hear and believe; none may claim ignorance of the Truth. As stated in *A Ray of Light*, "The message about Christ will be spread to all nations of the world; not one nation, or tribe, even in the farthest and unknown corners of the earth, will be left without the enlightenment of Christ's teaching. The last commandment of Jesus Christ will be fulfilled— *Go ye into all the world, and preach the gospel to every creature* (Mark 16:15)."[9]

The Book of Revelation portrays in a single sentence the outlines of sacred history in terms of Satan's initial free reign, his restriction during the Church age, his end-times release, and his ultimate doom: "The beast that you saw was, and is not, and will ascend out of the bottomless pit and go to perdition" (Revelation 17:8).

This vision came to Saint John the Theologian during his period of exile on the island of Patmos after Christ's Resurrection. At that time Satan, being in bondage, "is not." Prior to that, he "was," and at the end of the Church age, he "will ascend out of the bottomless pit." At Christ's Return he will "go to perdition."

Saint Andrew expanded on Saint John's vision as follows: "This beast is Satan who, having been put to death by the Cross of Christ, will again, as it is said, come back to life at the end. By false signs and miracles he will, through the Antichrist, act for the overthrowing of the Cross. Therefore he was and acted up to the time of the Cross and then he was no longer, inasmuch as by the saving passion he was made powerless and was deprived of the authority which he had over the peoples through idol worship."

Satan's thousand-year incarceration takes its place among the truly significant events in sacred history. Had it not happened, the earth would surely be unrecognizable today. Secular "history," ignoring Christ, cannot comprehend the spiritual reality which undergirds worldly happenings. Yet the signs of the last days will go unrecognized by those who lack a clear understanding of Satan's period of bondage. Why? Because eventually the evil one goes FREE!

[1] "Prayer to the Venerable Cross," *Prayer Book,* p. 58.
[2] "The Gospel of Nicodemus," ch. 8, in *The Ante-Nicene Fathers,* Vol. VIII, p. 437.
[3] *Orthodox Dogmatic Theology,* p. 343.
[4] *The City of God,* Book XX, ch. 9, pp. 725-728.
[5] *Prayer Book,* p. 50.
[6] *The Christian Tradition,* Vol. 1, p. 129.
[7] *Orthodox Dogmatic Theology,* pp. 344-345, footnote 4.
[8] *The Apocalypse of St. John,* p. 197.
[9] *A Ray of Light,* Archimandrite Panteleimon, comp., pp. 29-30.

Chapter 6

The Beginning of
the Last Days

*Who places earthly kings on their thrones? He
who alone sits on the throne of fire from eternity,
and alone, in the true sense, rules over all
creation. Authority, power, courage, and wisdom
is given the Czar from the Lord to govern his
subjects.*

— *Saint John of Kronstadt*

The prospect of Satan's thousand-year bondage eventually ending, even though for a short while, has worried people since before it began. It has been an ominous cloud on the horizon which has loomed larger and blacker with each passing century. Though the event was distant for them, the Bible's Prophets and Apostles described it in the direst terms: "That day is a day of wrath . . . a day of darkness and gloominess" (Zephaniah 1:15); "a time of trouble, such as never was since there was a nation, even to that time" (Daniel 12:1); "in the last days perilous times will come" (2 Timothy 3:1).

"The last days"—this one biblical phrase conjures up frightful images, and anxious people have predicted the "end of the world" throughout history. Although Christ said that the actual moment of His Return is a secret known only to God, the Holy Scriptures do offer specific guidance as to when the end times are to begin.

The Bible teaches that God assigned angels the task of binding Satan at the beginning of his thousand years in the bottomless pit: "Then I saw an angel coming down from heaven, having the key to the bottomless pit and a great chain in his hand. He laid hold of the dragon, that serpent of old, who is the Devil and Satan, and bound him for a thousand years" (Revelation 20:1, 2). Yet no angel is charged with *keeping* the serpent bound!

The Withholding One

Saint Paul revealed that it is actually a man (though one with a divine commission), not an angel, who is to restrain the evil one in his bondage. The Apostle further warned that this human guardian will eventually himself be removed, "taken out of the way," allowing the evil one to escape his prison: "Let no one deceive you by any means; for that Day will not come unless the falling away comes first, and the man of sin is revealed, the son of perdition, who opposes and exalts himself above all that is called God or that is worshiped. . . . And now you know what is restraining, that he may be revealed in his own time. For the mystery of lawlessness is already at work; only He [or *he*] who now restrains will do so until He [or *he*] is taken out of the way. And then the lawless one will be revealed" (2 Thessalonians 2:3-8).

While he is locked up, Satan's influence is limited and clandestine, "the mystery of lawlessness" [KJV, "iniquity"]. According to Father Seraphim Rose, it is called a mystery "because a mystery is something that is not fully revealed in this world, that comes from another world. The mystery of righteousness is the whole story of how God came from heaven and became incarnate in order to save us; and the mystery of iniquity is the opposite—it's a mystery coming up from hell that breaks into this world and changes it. This, therefore, is the mystery of lawlessness which is preparing the world for the coming of the 'man of lawlessness.' "[1]

Who Guards?

After the passage of a millennium, the withholding one is to be forcibly removed. Then Satan will be loosed for a "little while," as Saint John says in Revelation 20. This catastrophic event can be said to mark conclusively the beginning of the end, which will culminate with our Lord's Return and the Last Judgment.

Some have speculated that "he who restrains" is the Holy Spirit or the Church. But speaking of the Holy Spirit the Lord says, "And I will pray the Father, and He will give you another Helper, that He may abide with you forever" (John 14:16). And He further promises, "I will build My church, and the gates of Hades shall not prevail against it" (Matthew 16:18). These passages testify that neither the Holy Spirit nor the Church, which is His visible expression, can ever be "taken out of the way." Blessed Augustine also states, "There shall be a Church in this world even when the devil shall be loosed, as there has been since the beginning, and shall be always."[2]

Who, then, is this guardian, also described as the "seal" which the angel of Revelation 20:3 set upon Satan, "that he should deceive the nations no more till the thousand years were finished"? The first glimpse of him in manifest history came in the year A.D. 312, as the Roman Emperor Constantine led his troops into battle. Looking up, Constantine saw in the sky a glowing cross emblazoned with the words, "By This Sign, Conquer."

Though himself a pagan at the time, Constantine ordered that the sign of the cross be inscribed on the shields and banners of his army, which then went on to wage victorious campaigns against great odds. As a result, the emperor accepted Christ. He then moved his capital to Constantinople, the "second Rome," and created a government and a culture based upon Christian principles.

Birth of the Christian Monarchy

Thus, Constantine became the first Christian monarch, combining the authority of earthly kingship with the piety of Christian faith. "The Christian Emperor was not an ordinary ruler," wrote Father Michael Azkoul.

"He was *vicarius Christi*. His coronation was a sacrament, for he was anointed, as was Saul, David and Solomon, to protect and guide God's People. . . . His authority was not simply political or administrative but spiritual. He was expected to be holy that he might lead his nation into holiness."[3]

"[The emperor's] coronation," adds Arthur Penrhyn Stanley, Dean of Westminster Abbey, "was not a mere ceremony, but a historical occasion and solemn consecration. It was preceded by fasting and seclusion . . . [the emperor] reciting aloud the confession of the Orthodox Faith; himself alone on his knees, offering up the prayer of intercession for the Empire."[4]

The Christian monarchy nurtured a Christian society through a hierarchical authority based on divine order. Father Azkoul continues, "As Jesus Christ was both God and man, so Orthodox monarchical society likewise possessed two dimensions, one earthly and one heavenly, united as the two Natures in Christ. The *Basileus* or *Tsar*, the imperium, Emperor, represented the humanity of Christ and the priesthood or *sacerdotium* was the analogy of His Divinity. They collaborated in the perfection of Christian society even as 'the Whole Christ' works for the salvation of the world."[5]

Kings were not incidental—they were essential for a fully Christian society. And emperors were needed for a fully Christian empire. They helped to protect the Church from heresy and schism from within, as well as protecting the empire from domination by non-Christian invaders.

Governments reflect godliness or the lack thereof in their very structure, noted Saint Gregory the Theologian in the fourth century. "For Anarchy is a thing without order; and the Rule of Many is factious, and thus anarchical, and thus disorderly. . . . But Monarchy is that which we hold in honour."[6]

The Guardian Revealed

Constantine the Great thus became the first of the guardians who "seal" the mystery of iniquity. Saint John Chrysostom explained in the fifth century that the Christian monarch was in fact none other than the "restraining one" whom Saint Paul had referred to. "When Roman authority ceases," Chrysostom wrote, "then he [Antichrist] will come. And rightfully so, because as long as people will be afraid of this government, no one will hasten to submit himself to Antichrist; but after it has been destroyed, anarchy will abide, and he will strive to steal all, both human and divine authority."

Recently canonized Saint John Maximovitch, Bishop of San Francisco, characterized the imperial authority of the Christian monarchy as "lawful." It was established by God's Law, and it dispersed that Law to mankind. In the realm of human conduct, the condition of lawfulness versus lawlessness is probably the most visible difference between Christ and Antichrist.

"Before the advent of Antichrist," Saint John Maximovitch wrote, "there is already being prepared in the world the possibility of his appearance: *The mystery of iniquity doth already work* (II Thes. 2:7). The forces preparing for his appearance fight above all against the lawful Imperial authority. . . . St. John Chrysostom explains that the 'withholding one' is the lawful pious authority: such an authority fights with evil. For this reason the 'mystery,' already at work in the world, fights with this authority; it desires a lawless authority. When the 'mystery' decisively achieves that authority, nothing will any longer hinder the appearance of Antichrist."[7]

In the 1800s Saint Theophan the Recluse anticipated the evil which would attend the eventual loss of the Christian monarchy: "When the monarchy falls," he said, "and everywhere nations institute self-government (republics, democracies), then the Antichrist will be able to act freely. It will not be difficult for Satan to prepare voters to renounce Christ as experience taught us during the French Revolution. There will be no one to veto the movement. . . . Thus, when such a social order is instituted everywhere, making it easy for antichristian movements to appear, then the Antichrist will come forth."[8]

It is also instructive to note that Saint Hippolytus referred to the ten toes of Nebuchadnezzar's great image as democracies: "The ten toes of the image are equivalent to (so many) democracies."[9]

Growth of the Holy Church

The unprecedented integration of earthly and spiritual authority in the person of a Christian monarch had profound and far-reaching implications. Once "he who restrains" was a living, human reality, the Holy Church flourished. Christianity exploded into the world, being carried by zealous missionaries west to Ireland, north to Finland and Russia, east to Armenia, south to Africa, and to all points in between.

In the tenth century the Slavic Prince Vladimir accepted Christianity for himself and his people, and patterned the Russian nation after the Byzantine model. His countrymen so embraced the riches of the Faith that their land came to be called "Holy Rus."

For over a thousand years Constantinople remained the capital of the Eastern Christian world. Emperor succeeded emperor, and although some sullied their personal reputations, the monarchy itself never wavered.

In the fifteenth century, Islamic incursion into the ancient Christian domains grew relentlessly. One by one, Antioch, Alexandria and Jerusalem all fell into Moslem hands. Finally, Constantinople herself was under siege. On May 29, 1453, following a long and hard-fought battle, the city was taken and her last emperor, Constantine XI, died fighting.

Russia Becomes "Third Rome"

But the Christian monarchy was not lost. Being the spiritual heirs of Byzantium, the Russian royalty assumed the guardianship of Orthodox Christianity. Russia became the "third Rome," and her sovereigns received the anointing of the Holy Spirit to maintain order and peace in the world. The capital of the empire was moved to Moscow, and the emperor adopted for his symbol the Byzantine double-headed eagle and for his title, "tsar" (derived from the Roman "caesar").

So fundamental was the Christian monarchy for protecting the peoples of the earth during the Church age that history cannot be properly understood apart from it. The secular view of the emperor as a mere political or administrative head ignores his far more important function as spiritual guardian. For this reason Saint Paul urged the ancient Christians to pray "for kings and all who are in authority," so "that we [the citizens] may lead a quiet and peaceable life" (1 Timothy 2:2).

Without this spiritual perspective, the succession of monarchs—especially those who displayed incontestable shortcomings—will appear to be merely a ludicrous confusion of personal and national interests. "Only if we understand the unique place of the Christian Roman Empire in the divine Economy will the history of the Christian Church make any sense," cautioned Father Michael Azkoul. "Only then will the preeminent role of the emperor or king in that history be understandable."[10]

The events surrounding the monarchy's demise have been greatly misunderstood by secular historians. This is predictable, since they omit Christ as operative in the world of men. History is far more than a dateline of occurrences, however.

"History," wrote Father Seraphim Rose, ". . . is not a chronology of political or economic events; it is what happens in the souls of men, for good or evil, and only then is reflected in outward events. In the whole 19th century there were only two 'historical events': the progress of the worldwide Revolution, which is to say, the progress of unbelief in men's souls; and the attempt of one power to stop it: Orthodox Russia. . . . Similarly, in the 20th century only one historical event is very visible to us as yet: the progress of Revolutionary atheism (or *anti-theism*, to use the Socialist Proudhon's more accurate word) once it has come to power."[11]

The Mystery of Iniquity Strikes

Throughout the Church age, the mystery of iniquity worked subtly and insidiously to foster unbelief. Satanically inspired humanism, which had received such impetus during the Renaissance and Enlightenment, reached its nihilistic nadir in the early twentieth century in the form of atheistic communism. The utopian ideology which is at the root of communism, and in fact of most secular thought, is seldom clearly realized even by its adherents; it has become part of the unexamined ideological inheritance of the post-Enlightenment era.

"One has to realize what Communism is," insisted Father Seraphim Rose. "Not merely a power-mad political regime, but an ideological-religious system whose aim is to overthrow and supplant all other systems, most of all Christianity. Communism is actually a very powerful *heresy* whose central thesis . . . is chiliasm or millennialism: history is to reach its culmination in an indefinite state of earthly blessedness, a perfected mankind living in perfect peace and harmony."[12]

Communism specifically attacked the land which had most nearly retained her ancient Christian traditions—Holy Russia. Propaganda portrayed Bolshevism as a political/social uprising, which is what gullible individuals throughout the world still imagine it to have been. But the "revolution" was far more than this—it was actually a battle against Christianity.

The Bolsheviks hated not only the emperor, but everything he represented. They were not content to see him deposed, but wanted him and every member of his family killed, so that the ancient link of Christian monarchy extending back to Constantine the Great would be forever severed.

The Russian Revolution was clearly satanic, and its entire success depended on the extermination of the last Christian monarch. If communism had failed in Russia, it would have died the inglorious death it deserved.

The Last Tsar

The Russian emperor, Tsar Nicholas II, was a pious man whose Christian priorities were as misunderstood by Western observers as they were despised by Lenin. Following the monarchist tradition, he was, in the words of Saint John Maximovitch, "the bearer and incarnation of the Orthodox world-view that the Tsar is the servant of God, the anointed of God. . . . He was thoroughly penetrated by this awareness; he viewed his bearing of the Imperial crown as a service to God. . . . He was a living incarnation of faith in the Divine Providence that works in the destinies of nations and peoples and directs Rulers faithful to God into good and useful actions. Therefore he was intolerable for the enemies of faith and for those who strive to put human reasoning and human faculties above everything."[13]

The tsar attempted to resist the Revolution, but eventually his own people, beguiled by the intellectual darkness of communism, abandoned him. Thus, though most of the world was and still is ignorant of what really happened, the greatest calamity of modern times occurred on July 17, 1918, when Nicholas II and the entire royal family were assassinated.

Priest Paul Volmensky wrote that "the murder of Czar Martyr Nicholas II . . . is a precise indicator that Antichrist is at the door and behind him is the Second Coming of Christ and the Last Judgement. The 'withholder' has been *taken out of the way* and satan works unbridled."[14]

The Romanovs' murder was only the first gust of a storm of martyrdoms which would lash every land touched by communism. Father Gleb Yakunin, who personally suffered under the godless regime, wrote, "The meaning for world history of the martyr's death of the Imperial Family, something that likens it to the most significant Biblical events, consists of the fact that here the Constantinopolitan period of the existence of the Church of Christ comes to an end, and a new, martyric, apocalyptic age opens up. It is begun with the voluntary sacrifice of the last anointed Orthodox Emperor and his family."[15]

Archimandrite Constantine of Jordanville offers this opinion: "The fall of Russia signalled a beginning to the pre-Antichrist epoch through which we are currently living. This cataclysm did away with the 'restraining power' in the world, setting Satan free from his temporary ('thousand-year', as the Scriptures allegorically call it) bondage."[16]

Free At Last!

With the tsar's death, the "times of the Roman Empire" were "fulfilled." As the last Christian monarch in the unbroken line which stretched back to Con-stantine the Great, Nicholas II was in a sense a "star fallen from heaven." His demise opened the "bottomless pit" in which Satan had been bound.

Saint John the Theologian expressed this as follows: "And I saw a star fallen from heaven to the earth. To him was given the key to the bottomless pit. And he opened the bottomless pit, and smoke arose out of the pit like the smoke of a great furnace. So the sun and the air were darkened because of the smoke of the pit" (Revelation 9:1, 2).

No longer was the evil one restrained from the full exercise of his perverted will. All that he had striven to do surreptitiously could henceforth be done in broad daylight. Beguilement of individuals could escalate to wholesale deception of nations. "Now when the thousand years have expired," wrote Saint John, "Satan will be released from his prison and will go out to deceive the nations which are in the four corners of the earth, Gog and Magog, to gather them together to battle" (Revelation 20:7, 8).

The dragon was free at last, but "having great wrath, because he knows that he has a short time" (Revelation 12:12). He has only a little while to bring the world to a fever pitch of apostasy, degradation and violence through the person of Antichrist. As Archbishop Averky wrote, "By the 'loosing of Satan out of his prison' is to be understood the appearance of Antichrist before the end of the world. The liberated Satan will strive in the person of Antichrist to deceive all the nations of the earth."[17]

The First Victims

Although Satan will ultimately deceive the entire world, he is particularly vengeful toward his first victims, "Gog and Magog." These are the ancient tribes which flourished in the land we now call Russia. It is no surprise that the country which had both bound Satan and borne the Christian empire to its end would be the first to suffer his demonic wrath. Blessed Augustine also points out that these tribal names suggest that Satan is reclaiming his "house" in which he was bound so long: "The meaning of these names we find to be, Gog, 'a roof,' Magog, 'from a roof,'—a house, as it were, and he who comes out of the house. They are therefore the nations in which we found that the devil was shut up as in an abyss, and the devil himself coming out from them and going forth."[18]

Loving death, Satan has lost no time in gathering the nations "together to battle." Since the destruction of the monarchy, the world has suffered evil of such monstrous proportions that nothing in previous history compares to it. Daniel's prediction of "a time of trouble, such as never was since there was a nation, even to that time" (Daniel 12:1) has begun to come true with a vengeance. One generation has seen two world wars, innumerable and continuous smaller conflagrations, annihilation of entire cities with atomic bombs, mass murders of millions, Naziism, fascism, communism, virulent epidemics, and worldwide falling away from the Faith. It is more than evident that, as Father Michael Azkoul writes, "the fall of the Christian Roman Empire has wrought everywhere the collapse of civil and ecclesiastical order."[19]

The experience of Russia since 1917 illustrates in microcosm what the last days will bring to the entire world. "We can clearly see," wrote Monk Zachariah Liebmann, "that since the removal of 'he who restraineth' the power of Satan is no longer held back. We stand as horrified witnesses to the unleashing of evil which has occurred since 1917 in all aspects of life. The world is rushing to embrace and enthrone antichrist in a way that was not possible before. Instead of the visible manifestation of the One Holy Catholic and Apostolic Church on earth, we see warring 'jurisdictions' outstripping each other in worldliness . . . the selling out of the soul of the Church through 'Sergianism' and the ecumenical movement.

"In the world today examples of godlessness abound—nuclear weapons, dangerous genetics experiments, pollution, wars, famines and terrible new diseases. In the realm of morality, shameless excesses are committed. Millions of unborn children are slaughtered each year. Perversity has become an accepted 'choice.' Drug use is killing off young people, who are listening to so-called music with satanic overtones. And one could go on."[20]

The experience of Holy Russia may be unique, since it was an Orthodox Christian culture prior to the Bolshevik Revolution. A greater manifestation of evil was therefore required to overcome many centuries of devotion. Sadly, for most of the world, no such Christian depth exists. The harsh methods employed by communism are not required in today's spiritually tepid societies. Unbridled materialism and debauchery will serve nicely. Antichrist has many tools for binding mankind—"whatever makes you feel good" being the most effective.

"We're living in the last times," taught Father Seraphim Rose. "Antichrist is close, and what happens in Russia and other countries like it is the normal experience of our times. Here in the West we're living in a fool's paradise which can and probably will soon be lost. Let's start to prepare—not by storing food or such outward things that some are already doing in America, but with the inward preparation of Orthodox Christians."[21]

In the face of such signs and testimony, Christians should neither despair nor fear, however. The Lord has promised never to forsake His own, and to preserve them in all times of trouble. Armed with the sure knowledge that the last days have begun, and that all that has been prophesied will soon be fulfilled, Christians can prepare themselves to heed the Lord's admonition to watch and pray, "that you may be counted worthy to escape all these things that will come to pass" (Luke 21:36).

---

[1] Christensen, *Not of This World,* p. 997.

[2] *The City of God,* Book XX, ch. 8, p. 722.

[3] *Sacred Monarchy and the Modern Secular State,* pp. 10-11.

[4] Quoted by Paul Marshall Allen, *Vladimir Soloviev, Russian Mystic,* p. 4.

[5] *Sacred Monarchy and the Modern Secular State,* p. 4.

[6] Third Theological Oration, "On the Son," in *Nicene and Post-Nicene Fathers,* Vol. VII, p. 301.

[7] *The Last Judgement,* p. 176.

[8] *A Ray of Light,* Archimandrite Panteleimon, comp., p. 38.

[9] "Treatise on Christ and Antichrist," in *The Ante-Nicene Fathers,* Vol. V, p. 209.

[10] *Anti-Christianity: The New Atheism,* p. 102.

[11] *Not of This World,* p. 616.

[12] *Ibid.,* p. 379.

[13] *Tsar-Martyr Nicholas II,* pp. 1-2.

[14] "In Memory of the 75th Anniversary of the Murder of Czar Martyr Nicholas II," *Orthodox Life,* Vol. 43, No. 4, July-August 1993, pp. 2, 6.

[15] Quoted by Fr. Seraphim Rose, *Heavenly Realm,* p. 94.

[16] *Ecumenism, Communism and Apostasy,* p. 3.

[17] *The Apocalypse of St. John,* p. 202.

[18] *The City of God,* Book XX, ch. 11, p. 729.

[19] *Antichristianity: The New Atheism,* p. 103.

[20] "The Life of Tsar-Martyr Nicholas II," *The Orthodox Word*, Vol. 26, No. 4 (153), July-August 1990, pp. 223-224.

[21] *Not of This World*, p. 877.

Chapter 7

The Meaning of the Russian Miracle

It is not for us to enjoy ourselves, to amuse ourselves, to dance on the grave of Russia, brought down to its deathbed by us, but rather to repent in tears. . . .

—*Archbishop Averky*

For the first time in nearly a century, Russian Orthodox Christians officially celebrated Christ's Incarnation on January 7, 1992 (the Russian Church is on the Old Calendar). Christmas had not been permitted as a governmentally sanctioned holiday since the Bolshevik Revolution of 1917. This festival, representing religious freedom for millions of longsuffering people, captured the miraculous spirit of the times. It was a fitting culmination to the chain of events which had led beyond *glasnost* and *perestroika* to the utter collapse of the Soviet state.

The rapid and virtually wholesale demise of Soviet communism took most onlookers by surprise. As they had been powerless to cause, world leaders were equally powerless to forestall or slow the deterioration of the totalitarian system which had held millions hostage for decades.

It is tempting to consider the Soviet disintegration as a direct or implied victory for Western democracy and free-market capitalism. But while the economic, social and political shortcomings of communism are obvious, they could neither anticipate nor account for the complete upheaval of the regime which previously had jeopardized the entire planet.

No Surprises

Far deeper principles are at work in the "Russian miracle" than economics or politics. Yet these under-lying forces have remained undetected and unreported by secular observers because they are spiritual. Christians in Russia, on the other hand, are not surprised by what happened, since they predicted it long ago.

Russian visionaries before the revolution saw what was going to happen and why. They saw how their country's misery would begin, and how it would ultimately end. They perceived the monumental implications of all this for the entire world. And they completely understood that Russian history was bound up with the end times.

In 1905 Father John of Kronstadt, one of Russia's most beloved modern saints, emphatically warned, "Russia, if you fall away from your faith, as many of the intellectual class have already fallen away, you will no longer be Russia or Holy Russia. And if there will be no repentance in the Russian people—then the end of the world is near. God will take away the pious Tsar and will send a whip in the person of impious, cruel, self-appointed rulers, who will inundate the whole earth with blood and tears."[1]

These prophetic words were fulfilled in 1917, when Marxist philosophy and Leninist rhetoric so inflamed the Russian populace that many lost touch with their Orthodox Christian sensibilities. In the ensuing madness, Tsar Nicholas II and his entire family were brutally murdered, bringing to an end the succession of Christian monarchs that had begun in the fourth century with Constantine the Great. Over the next seventy years, millions of Christians were killed. The Church, along with the Christian culture it had nurtured for nearly a millennium, was ruthlessly persecuted.

Fount of Revolution

The Russian Revolution actually began in France. It was there the humanistic and utopian slogan of "liberty, equality, fraternity" was first used successfully to separate the populace from its Christian heritage. The chief target of the French Revolution was the monarchy, based as it was on Christian principles. By destroying this, the revolution endeavored to make man his own ruler, separating him (as a nation) from the protection of a king—and of the King of kings.

"Kingship and the idea of descending political power—that is, political power 'descending' from God to the king for the benefit of the people—finally expired with the 'republicanism' of the French Revolution," wrote Father Michael Azkoul. "1789 marks the traditional date for the beginning of the complete and radical secularization of the Western world. From this moment, 'democracy' becomes its political ideal and atheism its political consequence. God is forever shut off from human affairs, dying a quiet death in the scientific madness of the 19th century, with no one to grieve him, as Nietzsche moaned. Now the universe was in the hands of man and, as August Comte proclaimed, he was its 'god' and the love of humanity his religion."[2]

Bolshevism took its cues from the French Revolution, adopting many of the same objectives and methods, with the goal of establishing a totally secular and godless society. In Russia, however, the monarchy was not merely Christian in principle, but was the specific inheritor of the crown of Constantine, as well as the guardian of Orthodoxy. The tsar served as the "seal" of the mystery of lawlessness not merely for the Russian people, but for the world.

The Russian monarchs were aware of their responsibilities as spiritual guardians. Emperor Alexander III (who was called "the Peacemaker" not by the Russian people, but by Europe) said, "Should the autocracy collapse, God forbid, all of Russia will collapse with her. The fall of age-old Russian rule will bring about an endless era of discord and bloody civil wars."

The Coming Storm

The Christian monarchy had endured for 1600 years. Russia herself had been an Orthodox nation for over 900 years. Who could have anticipated the effect of a few madmen shouting Bolshevik slogans? Yet at Optina, Russia's most famous monastery, Starets (spiritual elder) Anatole the Younger of Optina made a drastic prediction: "There will be a storm. And the Russian ship will be smashed to pieces. But people can be saved even on splinters and fragments. And not everyone will perish."[3]

The starets' understated words all came to pass: countless innocent people died, while the very fabric of traditional Russian society was shredded. Not content with destroying the monarchy, the Marxists systematically exterminated millions of ordinary citizens in an effort to eradicate belief in God from the society. Optina Monastery was closed in 1925; the monks were forced out and the buildings condemned.

Yet even in the storm of satanic hatred, people were saved "on splinters and fragments." After the visible Church organization was corrupted to Marxist ends, many of the faithful met secretly in their homes and in the forests, reviving the "catacomb" traditions of the earliest Christians. "For Russia the times of the catacombs have been resurrected," wrote Saint John Maximovitch.[4]

Thousands of churches were destroyed or converted to profane uses, such as barns or offices. Communists confiscated the relics of long-venerated saints and either destroyed them or displayed them in "museums" as examples of supposedly ridiculous and antiquated superstitions. Yet all this was foreseen by Elder Barnabas of the Gethsemane Skete in the early 1900s: "Persecutions against the faith will constantly increase. There will be an unheard-of grief and darkness, and almost all the churches will be closed."[5]

Instead of the liberty and better life which the communist revolution deceitfully promised, it delivered its adherents to unprecedented bondage and misery. To the outward eye, Russia as it had been known for 900 years—that is, Holy Russia—was dead.

Rebirth Prophesied

But Elder Alexius of the Zosima Hermitage claimed otherwise: "Who is it that is saying that Russia is lost, that she has perished? No, no, she is not lost, she has not perished and will not perish."[6]

As the revolution took complete control of the country, the "impious, cruel, self-appointed rulers" submerged the populace beneath a deluge of deception. Lies and terror became the norm. Nevertheless, those with Christian understanding were not deceived. Not only had Russia not died, they said, but her suffering had profoundly religious implications. Russia's problems were not caused by economic imbalance, social unrest or political opportunism, but by the state of the nation's soul.

"The Russian people must be purified of sin through great trials," declared Elder Alexius. "One must pray and fervently repent. But Russia is not lost and has not perished."[7]

Porphyrius, an ascetic of Glinsk Monastery, declared in 1914 that simple believers would yet resurrect Russia: "But in defence of faith there will arise from among the people those who are unknown to the world and they will restore what has been trampled on."[8]

These Christian visionaries shared a clear awareness that Russia's misfortune was linked to the end times, and was in reality a preparation for the coming of the Antichrist. But rather than despair, they called their countrymen to repentance. In this they revealed that Russia's strength during those dark years lay not in her armies and nuclear warheads, but in the hearts of her Christian martyrs.

Schema-hieromonk Aristocleus promised in 1918, "Now we are undergoing the times before Antichrist, but Russia will yet be delivered. There will be much suffering, much torture. The whole of Russia will become a prison, and one must greatly entreat the Lord for forgiveness. One must repent of one's sins and fear to do even the least sin, but strive to do good, even the smallest. For even the wing of a fly has weight, and God's scales are exact. And when even the smallest of good in the cup overweighs, then will God reveal His mercy upon Russia."[9]

Eldress Agatha of Belo-Russia was an ascetic nun who had received a vision from the Mother of God in her youth. In the early 1930s she directed Christians to avoid the Soviet church: "This is not a true church," she said. "It has signed a contract to serve antichrist. Do not go to it. Do not receive any Mysteries from its servants. Do not participate in prayer with them. There will come a time when churches will be opened in Russia, and the true Orthodox faith will triumph. Then people will become baptized, as at one time they were baptized under St. Vladimir. When the churches are opened for the first time, do not go to them because these will not be true churches; but when they are opened the second time, then go—these will be the true churches. . . . The atheist Soviet authority will vanish, and all its servants will perish."[10]

It was evident to some that Russia's penance and repentance would have worldwide implications. In 1917 Father Paul Florensky wrote, "I am convinced that the worst lies before us, and not behind us. . . . But I believe that this crisis will purify the Russian atmosphere, even the atmosphere of the entire world."[11]

As communism spread like a plague into Eastern Europe, Asia, and the Americas, those who were able to flee their oppressed homelands also filtered into other countries. As a result of this dispersal, an even broader spiritual significance of the revolution became discernible: "In chastising, the Lord at the same time also shows the Russian people the way to salvation by making it a preacher of Orthodoxy in the whole world," wrote Saint John Maximovitch. "The Russian Diaspora has made all the ends of the world familiar with Orthodoxy; the mass of Russian exiles, for the most part, is unconsciously a preacher of Orthodoxy. . . . To the Russians abroad it has been granted to shine in the whole world with the light of Orthodoxy, so that other peoples, seeing their good deeds, might glorify our Father Who is in heaven, and thus obtain salvation for themselves."[12]

Communism's Collapse

After seventy years of spiritual and material deprivation, the masses of Soviet people had reached a state of numb hopelessness. It was impossible to imagine any power or circumstance great enough to break the communist stronghold. Many Westerners also considered the Soviet Union a virtually unbeatable entity, a conscienceless superpower whose motto, "We will bury you!" was a permanently chilling possibility. As country after country succumbed to the socialist onslaught, the communist advance seemed to be inexorable. Yet the God-inspired Russian luminaries who had foreseen the birth of communism foresaw also its later collapse and aftermath.

In 1918 Schema-hieromonk Aristocleus, referring to the ultimate death of Bolshevism, declared, "There will be an extraordinary outburst and a miracle of God would be manifested. And there will be an entirely different life, but all this will not be for long."[13]

Elder Barnabas of the Gethsemane Skete spoke in terms of a "deliverance" which would be short-lived, a mere "flowering" before the end: "But when it will seem to people that it is impossible to endure any longer, then deliverance will come. But this will be a flowering before the end."[14]

After the "storm" of communism, God will miraculously restore Russia, explained Starets Anatole the Younger in 1917: "And what happens after a storm? . . . There will be a calm. . . . A great miracle of God will be manifested. And all the splinters and fragments [of the smashed 'Russian ship'], by the will of God and his power, will come together and be united, and the ship will be rebuilt in its beauty and will go on its own way as foreordained by God. And this will be a miracle evident to everyone."[15]

Elder Nectarius of Optina predicted in the 1920s that not only would Russia be freed from her oppressors, but that as a result of repentance, she would become spiritually rich. "Russia will arise, and materially it will not be wealthy. But in spirit it will be wealthy, and in Optina there will yet be seven luminaries, seven pillars."[16]

In 1987 Optina was in fact reopened, and repairs were begun following its extensive destruction and desecration. A Moscow University student later verified the accuracy of Elder Nectarius' prophetic words: "Now I see that all our history, arts, customs and even language are built on Orthodox Christianity. If we safeguard our Orthodoxy, we are the richest nation, even if we are economically poor. Orthodoxy is Russia's most precious treasure."[17]

Return of the Tsar?

For Russians, the greatest sin on the national conscience has been that of regicide. Tsar Nicholas II, the servant of Christ, had been abandoned by his own people to be butchered by the communists. As Father Gleb Yakunin lamented, "The tragedy of the Royal Family has lain like a curse on the Russian land, having become the symbolic prologue of Russia's long path of the Cross— the death of tens of millions of her sons and daughters. The canonization of the Imperial Martyrs will be for Russia the lifting from her of the sin of regicide; this will finally deliver her from the evil charms."[18]

As if in response to the reviving Russian national contrition, in 1979 a startling discovery was made. Researcher Geli Ryabov located, after extensive secret investigations, the buried relics of Tsar Nicholas II. Nine skeletons were dug up from a pit in Ekaterinburg, where the royal family had been killed.[19] This had a profound impact on the nation. Informed sources report that "gradually the Russian conscience has begun to awaken. Memorial services to the Tsar have been held across the country. . . . Voices in the Russian press have openly brought up the question of 'national guilt' for the death of their Tsar, which they say must somehow, through acts of repentance, be expiated."[20]

Could such repentance herald the reinstatement of the Christian monarchy? The *Atlanta Journal/Constitution* reported on July 7, 1991, that a descendant of Michael Romanov, Russia's first Romanov tsar, was discovered living in exile in Paris, and that Russian monarchists had elected regents to represent him.

Regarding the return of a tsar, Archbishop Theophan of Poltava wrote in 1930, "The coming of Antichrist draws nigh and is very near. The time separating us from him should be counted a matter of years and at most a matter of some decades. But before the coming of Antichrist Russia must yet be restored—to be sure, for a short time. And in Russia there must be a Tsar forechosen by the Lord Himself. He will be a man of burning faith, great mind and iron will. This much has been revealed about him."[21]

When so many of the predictions of righteous Russian sufferers have come to pass, all their words must take on added importance. A theme repeated by many is that the restoration of Russia will be temporary. It will be a "flowering before the end," a brief return to true Christian beliefs and practices. And it will presage a wave of worldwide repentance prior to the appearance of Antichrist.

Heavenly Silence

Father Seraphim Rose linked Revelation's "heavenly silence" to Russia's period of quiet before the final storm: "In the book which most thoroughly describes the events to occur at the end of the world, the *Apocalypse* of St. John the Theologian, at the opening of the seventh seal, which precedes the final plague to come upon mankind, it is said that there was silence in heaven for the space of half an hour (Apoc. 8:1). Some have interpreted this to mean a short period of peace before the final events of world history—namely . . . when the preaching of world-wide repentance will begin with Russia."[22]

This repentance is a sign that evil, regardless of its apparent power, is not stronger than good. Satan can and will be defeated, but only by those who are willing to suffer for Christ. Those who endure crucifixion for the Lord's sake will certainly be resurrected. "It is a law of the spiritual life that where there is Golgotha—if it is genuine suffering for Christ—there will be resurrection," Father Seraphim Rose assures us. "This resurrection first of all occurs in human hearts, and we do not need to be too concerned what outward form it might take by God's will. All signs point to the fact that we are living at the end of the world, and any outward restoration of Holy Orthodox Russia will be short-lived."[23]

The world at large gloats over communism's apparently untimely end and rewards itself with complacency. It has no idea that the fractured societies left in communism's wake are but decoys, left to divert suspicion from the true arena of conflict. The revolution is not over, nor have we in the West "won," for the battle is ultimately spiritual in nature.

Marx's "opiate of the masses" is in reality his own nihilistic belief that this present life is all there is. Toxic and addictive, it is a deadening aroma that has spread beyond the fevered minds of communist plotters to infiltrate nearly every arena of human thought and enterprise. Examine the media, the schools, the government, and then ask: Did they not bury us, after all? What the political revolution has failed to do, and perhaps was never really expected to do, has been effectively achieved by more "delicate" means.

"Communism in its crude primitive form of militant atheistic materialism will outlive itself, giving place to more subtle forms of struggle with Christ," wrote Archimandrite Constantine. "In so doing, it will bring us right up to the manifestation of the Antichrist in its final concrete form."[24]

Sober Christians must reject the complacency in which the ignorant indulge. The downfall of Russian communism is no license for ease-taking, but an eloquent harbinger of the end. It is a sign that all is being fulfilled just as prophets, apostles and Christian visionaries throughout the ages have foretold. Every day, every second, draws us nearer to the final contest between our Lord and His enemies.

The ultimate Victor, of course, has already won, and the ultimate loser has already lost. Indeed, the only remaining question is: Who among mankind will make the hard choice of remaining loyal to Christ in a world culture given over to Antichrist?

In these culminating moments, perhaps the Russian martyrs may yet instruct us, with their example of preferring death to deceit, firing squads to faithlessness. If so, their sacrifice will serve us even as it saved them. And if, as a result of the testimony of their suffering, others find the strength to live and the courage to die for Christ, then truly the Russian miracle will belong to all.

[1] *Father John of Kronstadt*, 50th Anniversary Book, Utica, N.Y., 1958, p. 164, as quoted by Fr. Seraphim Rose, *Heavenly Realm*, p. 88.

[2] *Sacred Monarchy and the Modern Secular State,* p. 5.

[3] *Orthodox Russia,* 1970, No. 1, p. 9, as quoted in *Heavenly Realm,* p. 89.

[4] *A New Age of Martyrs and Catacombs,* p. 3.

[5] Private letter from N. Kieter, as quoted in *Heavenly Realm,* p. 90.

[6] *Orthodox Russia,* 1970, No. 1, p. 9, as quoted in *ibid.,* p. 89.

[7] *Ibid.*

[8] I.M. Andreyev, *Russia's Catacomb Saints,* p. 526.

[9] *Orthodox Russia,* 1969, No. 21, p. 3, as quoted in *Heavenly Realm,* p. 90.

[10] By the late 1930s nearly all churches in Russia were closed. Stalin opened the churches "for the first time," during World War II, then closed them again. The second opening occurred following communism's demise.

[11] Private letter to A. S. Mamontov.

[12] *The Orthodox Word,* 1973, No. 50, pp. 92, 94, as quoted in *Heavenly Realm,* p. 99.

[13] *Orthodox Russia,* 1969, No. 21, p. 3, as quoted in *ibid.,* p. 91.

[14] Private letter from N. Kieter, as quoted in *ibid.,* p. 90.

[15] *Orthodox Russia,* 1970, No. 1, p. 9, as quoted in *ibid.,* pp. 89-90.

[16] *Optina Monastery and Its Epoch,* p. 538, as quoted in *ibid.,* p. 91.

[17] "Letter from Russia," *Orthodox America,* Vol. XIII, No. 8, May-June 1993, p. 8.

[18] *La Pense Russe,* Dec. 6, 1979, No. 3285, p. 50, as quoted in *Heavenly Realm,* p. 94.

[19] *The Atlanta Journal/Constitution,* June 23, 1992, p. A2.

[20] *The Orthodox Word,* Vol. 26, No. 4 (153), July-August 1990, p. 220.

[21] *The Orthodox Word,* 1969, No. 5, p. 194, as quoted in *Heavenly Realm,* p. 91.

[22] *Heavenly Realm,* p. 98.

[23] Christensen, *Not of This World,* p. 882.

[24] *Ecumenism, Communism and Apostasy,* p. 14.

Chapter 8

The Spirit of the End Times

Fear hypocrisy: fear it precisely because it is in the character of the times and is able to infect everyone at the smallest deviation into lightminded conduct.
      —*Saint Tikhon of Zadonsk*

The traumatic mood of the end times is captured succinctly in the word "trouble." Israel's Prophets spoke apprehensively of the agitation which is to precede the Lord's Second Coming: "At that time . . . there shall be a time of trouble, such as never was since there was a nation, even to that time" (Daniel 12:1).

The Prophets looked ahead to "the day of the Lord," when Christ would return, with foreboding: "Wail, for the day of the LORD is at hand!" cried Isaiah. ". . . Therefore all hands will be limp, every man's heart will melt, and they will be afraid" (Isaiah 13:6-8).

"That day is a day of wrath," warned Zephaniah, "a day of trouble and distress, a day of devastation and desolation, a day of darkness and gloominess, a day of clouds and thick darkness" (Zephaniah 1:15).

Amos warned those who claimed to be eager for that day to come that the brightness of God would make sinful man seem dark by comparison: "Woe to you who desire the day of the LORD!" admonished Amos. ". . . It will be darkness, and not light" (Amos 5:18).

Malachi likened the Lord's day to an oven. This idea persists throughout the Scriptures, as God is called a "consuming fire," whose "light" either illumines or burns. "For behold, the day is coming, burning like an oven" (Malachi 4:1).

That the fire of God will destroy much goes without saying, for in the end times the world will have rejected its Creator, and there will be little worth saving. "Alas for the day!" wept Joel. "For the day of the LORD is at hand; it shall come as destruction from the Almighty" (Joel 1:15).

Israel's Prophets spoke of these troubles afflicting not only human society, but even the natural world. The earth will tremble from storms and convulsions. Devastating sickness will spread through populations. Senseless wars and other manmade disasters will create misery and agony. Yet all these, as Jesus warned, signal merely the beginning.

"And you will hear of wars and rumors of wars. See that you are not troubled; for all these things must come to pass, but the end is not yet. For nation will rise against nation, and kingdom against kingdom. And there will be famines, pestilences, and earthquakes in various places. All these are the beginning of sorrows" (Matthew 24:6-8).

"Before the end of life on earth there will be agitation, wars, civil war, hunger, earthquakes," wrote Saint John Maximovitch. "Men will suffer from fear, will die from expectation of calamity. There will be no life, no joy of life, but a tormented state of falling away from life. But there will be a falling away not only from life, but from faith also, and *when the Son of Man cometh, shall He find faith on the earth?* (St. Luke 18:8)."[1]

Perilous Times

Man has believed the lie. He has not only eaten the forbidden fruit, but justified his disobedient act. He has become the ultimate dupe: an apologist for Satan. He has rejected the Kingdom of God in order to reign over a pathetic little world of corruption. He has enslaved heart and soul in order to experience the passions of his fallen mind and body. He has denied virtue, and been eaten up by vice. He has craved immortality, but only of the flesh.

"But know this," predicted Saint Paul two millennia ago, "that in the last days perilous times will come: For men will be lovers of themselves, lovers of money, boasters, proud, blasphemers, disobedient to parents, unthankful, unholy, unloving, unforgiving, slanderers, without self-control, brutal, despisers of good, traitors, headstrong, haughty, lovers of pleasure rather than lovers of God, having a form of godliness but denying its power" (2 Timothy 3:1-5).

Truth has been not only rejected, but mocked: "Scoffers will come in the last days, walking according to their own lusts," wrote Saint Peter (2 Peter 3:3). Saint Jude described the same thing: "The apostles of our Lord Jesus Christ . . . told you that there would be mockers in the last time who would walk according to their own ungodly lusts. These are sensual persons, who cause divisions, not having the Spirit" (Jude 17-19).

Having lost the ability to discern right from wrong, many have turned, "as a dog returns to his own vomit" (Proverbs 26:11), to pagan idols. Proponents of the "New Age," for example, offer nothing at all new, but a restoration of demon worship by means of fanciful "spiritual" guides promoting a plethora of heathen teachings. "For the time will come," Saint Paul foresaw, "when they will not endure sound doctrine, but according to their own desires, because they have itching ears, they will heap up for themselves teachers; and they will turn their ears away from the truth, and be turned aside to fables" (2 Timothy 4:3, 4).

What Is Truth?

Pilate's great question has been dismissed as irrelevant. Truth is no longer a subject of legitimate enquiry. Having willfully closed the doors on authentic understanding, mankind's only option is to devise his own "virtual" reality. Modern thought reflects this degeneration, having been reduced, in Father Seraphim

Rose's words, to "an experiment in the possibilities of knowledge open to man, assuming that *there is no Revealed Truth.* . . . The conclusion of this experiment is an absolute negation: if there is no Revealed Truth, there is no truth at all."[2]

In rejecting truth, man, being made in God's image, has denied himself. He has willfully blinded himself to reality, the conclusive foolhardy act: "The fool has said in his heart, 'There is no God' " (Psalm 14:1). For if there is no truth (often expressed more palatably as "all truth is relative"), then there can be no Christ God, who alone is "the way, the truth, and the life" (John 14:6).

It could be reasoned that the rejection of truth is at the heart of all demonic doctrines, for when the serpent contested God's word, saying to Eve, "You will not surely die" (Genesis 3:4), was he not lying as well as claiming *God* had lied? Jesus called Satan a liar from the beginning, and Saint Paul understood the clear relationship between the false doctrines of demons and the loss of faith: "Now the Spirit expressly says that in latter times some will depart from the faith, giving heed to deceiving spirits and doctrines of demons" (1 Timothy 4:1).

People who deny truth, and thus their own nature, inexorably become either suicidal or anarchistic. To all who think through the implications of the Lie, a brutal logic emerges: Why endure the "thousand natural shocks that flesh is heir to," as Shakespeare put it,[3] if life has no meaning? If there is nothing beyond the grave, no reward or punishment to come, why exercise self-restraint or show concern for others? Clearly, if there is no truth, then all things are lawful (which merely means, nothing is unlawful). By this reasoning one should seize all possible pleasure regardless of cost, or else put oneself beyond the reach of problems through self-extinction!

If man is not immortal, if there is no truth, then there can be no salvation. A society in denial becomes a society in despair. And if man has lost even the inclination "to be saved and to come to the knowledge of the truth" (1 Timothy 2:4), what purpose does earthly life serve? Indeed, it has forfeited its justification for existence, claimed Archimandrite Constantine: "If the sole basis on which the New Testament world exists [is rejected]—that is, if humanity has ceased to accept for its own benefit the world-saving sacrifice of our Lord Jesus Christ—then, to a Christian awareness, the immediate trend of such a world toward its end is axiomatic. From this point of view, then, it is possible to say that each year which elapses brings us noticeably closer to the Last Judgment. It shows a progressive paralysis of the human will to be saved."[4]

Archimandrite Panteleimon agrees, stating, "When the Gospel . . . attracts all those capable of accepting its message and being reborn through the grace of the Holy Spirit, then there will be no more reason for the present order to continue. The end of the world will come."[5]

Nihilistic Fervor

The philosophical rejection of truth corresponds to a theological rejection of the source of truth, God. Nihilism—the belief in nothing—is the spiritual antithesis of belief in a heavenly Father. The permeation of this pseudophilosophy into human society has proceeded most efficiently within scientific spheres of thought, where man's desire to define life in terms of himself is seemingly legitimized by the conceit of objectivity.

A universe (as well as a man) without God can only be an accidental arrangement of immense statistical improbability. Yet the secular scientific mind regards the unlikely scenario of a self-starting and self-maintaining cosmos as the only possibility, the alternative being "unthinkable." In this dreary conception, an unsympathetic, horizonless vortex, having come from nowhere, speeds forever into the darkness toward . . . nothing. By utter chance it spawns mankind. By even greater chance this mankind becomes conscious. Eventually, the newly awakened child of the stars realizes that it is fatherless—a cosmic orphan, lost in the void.

"Whither do we move?" wailed Nietzsche. "Away from all suns? Do we not dash on unceasingly? Backwards, sideways, forewards, in all directions? Is there still an above and below? Do we not stray, as through infinite nothingness? Does not empty space breathe upon us? Has it not become colder? Does not night come on continually, darker and darker?"[6]

Nietzsche, who ended his life in madness, demonstrated that no sentient being can endure the full awareness (though false) of such absolute abandonment. Misery loves company—thus the emotive force which energizes worldly expressions of "concern for humanity," and other such inconsistencies. For if man is in fact an "orphan," orbiting pathetically in a universe whose depth does not extend beyond chemical formulations and electromagnetic frequencies, the illusion of love may deaden his pain temporarily, but it will bring no real surcease or consolation. The nothingness from which he emerges and to which he belongs will eventually destroy him.

Nihilism therefore contrives a convoluted and utterly improbable rationale: Though man's life is pointless, both individually and collectively, in bravely facing his meaningless existence he shall somehow experience titanic pride, lofty joy . . . even brotherly love!

Nineteenth-century Russian novelist Fyodor Dostoevsky mockingly portrayed this irrational expectation in his novel, *The Brothers Karamazov:* "Once humanity to a man renounces God (and I believe that period, analogous with the geological periods, will come to pass) the whole of the old outlook on life will collapse by itself . . . and, above all, the old morality, too, and a new era will dawn. Men will unite to get everything life can give, but only for joy and happiness in this world alone. Man will be exalted with a spirit of divine, titanic pride, and the man-god will make his appearance. Extending his conquest over nature infinitely every hour by his will and science, man will every hour by that very fact feel so lofty a joy that it will make up for all his old hopes of the joys of heaven. Everyone will know that he is mortal, that there is no resurrection, and he will accept death serenely and proudly like a god. His pride will make him realize that it's no use protesting, that life lasts only for a fleeting moment, and he will love his brother without expecting any reward. Love will satisfy only a moment of life, but the very consciousness of its momentary nature will intensify its fire to the same extent as it is now dissipated in the hopes of eternal life beyond the grave."[7]

The human soul is by nature Christian, as Tertullian pointed out in the second century. Rebellion against God is not natural to man, but rather is fostered by the Arch-rebel, Satan.

And great has been the success of this rebellion! There is virtually no organization in the world which does not now subscribe, at least implicitly, to Nietzsche's axiom: "There must be many kinds of 'truths,' and consequently there can be no truth. . . . Truth is ugly."[8]

Yet nihilism is seen most acutely in modern man himself, who, molded by his credo of nothingness, has lost all touch with a life of sanctity and craves only the realization of his darkest pleasures. Having lost true identity as a unique creation of God, the nihilist no longer possesses himself or his thoughts. His mentors are demonic creations of subhuman intellect, and he believes perversion to be normalcy. While he foolishly imagines himself to have achieved final freedom of will, he has in fact been emptied of any real self-determination.

Nihilism and the Unclean Spirit

Satan had his stronghold in the world before Christ's Incarnation and Resurrection. Then, during the "thousand-year" period when the son of perdition was bound, the gospel of Christ spread and cleansed the earth. Applying one of Christ's parables to this modern world, one could deduce that the evil which existed before Christ's Advent has multiplied *seven times* since Satan's release!

As explained in Chapter 5, Christ referred to the world as Satan's "house." Following the Lord's Resurrection, the strong man (Satan) was bound and his house spoiled during the Church age (Matthew 12:29). But after the unclean spirit is freed, it says, " 'I will return to my house from which I came.' And when he comes, he finds it empty, swept, and put in order. Then he goes and takes with him seven other spirits more wicked than himself, and they enter and dwell there; and the last state of that man is worse than the first. So shall it also be with this wicked generation" (Matthew 12:44, 45).

Nihilism has created the nothingness into which these spirits are invited. A house that is swept and emptied of Christian principles is totally vulnerable to the multiple wickednesses of Satan, who is filled with "great wrath" because of his limited time to do evil.

Lawlessness

Nihilism produces lawlessness, the most distinctive outward characteristic of the end times. Lawlessness is manifested as anarchy, or malevolent order. Although anarchy may appear chaotic, it has in fact an ordering principle: the denial of truth. Rejection of Christ results not in "nothingness," but in Antichrist.

Christ and Antichrist have always been and will always be the only choices. Nor is it possible to be in both camps at once, because "no one can serve two masters" (Matthew 6:24). Fence-straddlers who imagine that they are maintaining some kind of "objective" stance have already landed in the enemy's court. "He who is not with Me is against Me," warned Jesus (Luke 11:23).

Anarchy represents the total separation of the material from the spiritual world. No divine principles of any kind are acknowledged, personally or corporately. All law is considered arbitrary, even "natural" law. It is to be obeyed only when convenient or under threat of temporal punishment.

Lawlessness takes many forms, wreaking violence against basic human nature. Lactantius pointed out that in the last days "neither sex nor infancy will be spared. All things will be confused and mixed together contrary to the divine law and to the laws of nature."[9] This well describes modern attitudes tolerating aberrations such as homosexuality and voluntary abortion.

By contrast, the Orthodox Christian recognizes even in man's law (when fairly conceived and applied) the reflection of God's higher ordering principles. Jesus by no means abridged divine law, but completed it, as He said: "Do not think that I came to destroy the Law or the Prophets. I did not come to destroy but to fulfill" (Matthew 5:17).

The Orthodox Christian recognizes that natural laws are governed by an omniscient and omnipotent God, and he consequently desires human government which corresponds with the divine intelligence. The anarchist, refusing to acknowledge God, neither wants nor finds heavenly order. He reproduces the confusion of his mind in the external world, and conceives ultimately of a universe whose purpose and end are merely absurd.

Utopian Dreams

Flight from God produces in worldly man a desire to build on earth the paradise which he has rejected in heaven. Utopian ideals have galvanized human thought throughout history. Eve's temptation had utopian roots (springing as it did from Satan, the ultimate utopian)—the promise of a life in which man, not God, ruled. One of the most obvious utopian schemes portrayed in Holy Scripture was the Tower of Babel. The failure of this enterprise established an archetype for man's inability to create a successful surrogate of his true heavenly home.

Man has never been able to devise his own earthly paradise. Every attempt has crumbled, for the Garden has been cordoned off by a legion of angels. And the perfection man seeks cannot be found or created by him in this world. As Father Seraphim Rose explained, "God's creation is imperfect, for if it were perfect men would be satisfied with it alone and not led by its 'broken' character to what must be above it. . . . Man can rest only in God, so God alone is perfect, and the imperfections of the world and of men only lead us to what is truly perfect. Modern man, however, wants to rest in this world, so he has to make it perfect; since it obviously is not he must make it so. Hence the ideal, utopian character of all rational schemes of the world. . . . The choice before man is always the same: perfection in this world, or perfection in the other world. Man is not made to be able to live without the hope of some kind of perfection. For modern man, then, the choice is: the rationalist utopia, or God."[10]

Paradoxically, utopia offers nothing "new" to those seeking satisfaction on this earth, but rather a hopelessly distorted and imperfect version of the divine order. Yet foolish man continues to imagine that he can achieve the impossible: create his own heaven and be its god. Whenever he actually establishes (always temporarily) some kind of utopian society, however, its members are inevitably and inexorably reduced to a sublife of spiritual and social impoverishment.

For Christians, utopia is usually based on the notion that Christ will return and establish a thousand-year earthly kingdom for His saints. This idea, called chiliasm or millenarianism, is hardly novel, having been thoroughly examined at the Second Ecumenical

Council in the year 381 and condemned as a superstitious aberration.

Many Protestant commentators consider chiliastic proclivities to be within the normal range of opinion and speculation, thus revealing their estrangement from the wisdom of Apostolic Tradition. But the Fathers of the Church branded this teaching as a heresy precisely because it is *dangerous!*

"This false teaching wreaks terrible harm," wrote Archbishop Averky, "lulling to sleep the spiritual vigilance of the faithful and suggesting to them that the end of the world is far away (if in fact there will be an end), and therefore there is no particular need to *watch and pray,* to which Christ the Saviour constantly called His followers (*cf* Mt. 26:41), since everythin[g in the] world is gradually getting better and better, spiritual progress keeping step with materialism."[11]

Orthodoxy teaches that chiliastic ideas are heretical—based on Satan's age-old rebellion against God. According to Father Michael Pomazansky, "If it was at one time possible to express chiliastic ideas as private opinions, this was only until the Ecumenical Church expressed its judgment about this. But when the Second Ecumenical Council (381), in condemning all the errors of the heretic Apollinarius, condemned also his teaching of the thousand-year reign of Christ and introduced into the very Symbol of Faith the words concerning Christ: *And His Kingdom will have no end*—it became no longer permissible at all for an Orthodox Christian to hold these opinions."[12]

Secular utopians want to build an earthly kingdom; "Christian" utopians want Christ to deliver one to them. Both groups are really on the same side of the fence. Christ's Kingdom, by distinction, is not of this world—it never has been and never will be.

Whereas Christ offers His servants a perfect Kingdom in heaven, the Antichrist offers his servants the *promise* (which cannot be fulfilled) of a supposedly perfect kingdom in this world. Modern man, having lost touch with the spiritual reality upon which this earth is founded, has ceased to struggle for his heavenly homeland and given himself over to the easy path of staying where all his worldly friends are.

The Revolution

The currents of thought which make up nihilism, anarchism, utopianism and chiliasm have coalesced into a popular movement which its adherents unabashedly call "the Revolution." Not surprisingly, Satan's 1917 release from bondage coincided with an outburst of "revolutionary" rhetoric and ideology.

The Revolution dates at least back to Jewish Pharisaism (for the Jews wanted Christ to be an earthly king). This red thread of rebellion can be traced throughout history, where it has insinuated itself over time into incidents and institutions worldwide. The Revolution can now be discerned in the arts, science, education, religion, and of course, in politics.

The Revolution is, in its essence, rebellion against all lawful authority. God, governments, parents, husbands—all forms of divinely established authority have been subjected to revolutionary persecution. Father Seraphim Rose describes modern history as nothing more than "the chronicle of the fall of every authority."[13]

The goal of the Revolution is to obliterate all convictions based on truth and to create a "value-neutral" public consciousness. Referring again to the Lord's parable (Matthew 12:44), it is to sweep and empty the world of sanctity, in order that the seven wicked spirits of the end times can enter in. "The fundamental task of the servants of the coming Antichrist," taught Archbishop Averky, "is to destroy the old world with all its former concepts and 'prejudices' in order to build in its place a new world suitable for receiving its approaching 'new owner' who will take the place of Christ for people and give them on earth that which Christ did not give them."[14]

Revolutionary Workers

The servants of the Revolution, in whatever arena, are actually serving Antichrist. In his *Moralia,* sixth-century Pope Saint Gregory the Great described the way Antichrist gathers workers. "He captures all men whom he discovers living a carnal existence. Before he has manifested himself, he drags innumerable carnal men; yet he does not succeed in dragging them all because each day, thanks to penance and prayer, some return to a life of justice. Nevertheless, if he still captures innumerable persons, while he is not yet present in the world as a person, it is because there go before him evil agents who sow and scatter the paralyzing seeds of his wicked kingdom."[15]

Many people work for the Revolution without actually realizing the dark intelligence behind it, imagining themselves to be "original" by following inner "inspirations." There are others who, like Faust, consciously "sell their souls" to the devil. In either case, having renounced truth, such revolutionaries can no longer discern right from wrong, and are vulnerable to any demonic suggestion.

The first goal of the Revolution is to fracture all orderly societies on the anvil of anarchy. Yet once the world is transformed into a lawless desert, the Revolution anticipates an even greater accomplishment: the transformation of man. This "New Human Order" was crudely prefigured by Hitler and Mussolini, who envisioned a humanity pathetically reduced and reconstructed—force-fit into the Brave New World.

The shape into which the nihilist will ultimately be remolded is the reverse of his native birthright. He was created in God's image, but is being reformed into the image of Satan. Even now his natural appearance is mutating, as many children's humanoid/robotic/demonic "toys" suggest, into something subhuman.

Saint Nilus, a monk of Mount Athos, anticipated this incredible development in the nineteenth century: "The people of that time will be unrecognizable. When the time of the appearance of Antichrist will be near, people's reason will be darkened because of carnal sins; criminality and impiety will increase more and more. The world will become unrecognizable; people's appearance will change, and it will be impossible to distinguish men from women because of the shamelessness in fashions and hair styles. These people will become coarse, wild, and cruel, like animals because of the temptations of Antichrist. There will be no respect for parents and elders, love will disappear.

"Then Christian tradition and manners will change. Modesty and chastity will disappear; instead, fornication and dissipation will reign among the people. Deceit and avarice will reach unbelievable levels. . . . Fornication, adultery, homosexuality, crafty deeds, theft, and murder will dominate society. . . . The Church of God will be deprived of God-fearing pastors."

Stopping Apostasy

Some may entertain the hope that the tide can be turned—that the world's ills can be healed and even a kind of righteousness established. After all, the ideal of a new world order based on peace and understanding does seem on the surface to be a positive goal even Christians could support. But, like everything associated with the Antichrist, it is a deceptive proposition, a unification at the lowest possible level.

The unity espoused leaves the only real Unifier, Christ, out of the picture. Consequently whatever organization emerges from this effort will subjugate rather than elevate, for this is what the world does best.

The Scriptures caution that the tide of apostasy, ultimately, cannot be turned—that there will be no surcease, but rather a continual increase, of troubles in the world until the Antichrist himself appears. "And in the latter time of their kingdom, when *the transgressors have reached their fullness,* a king shall arise, having fierce features, who understands sinister schemes" (Daniel 8:23, emphasis added).

The world is terminally ill because it has rejected God. No human action can save it, and even the Lord declared, "I do not pray for the world" (John 17:9). Only the Return of Jesus Christ in glory will calm the wind and water which threaten to capsize believers. Until then, Alexander Kalomiros explains, "any attempt on the part of Christians to change the course the world has taken would be futile and ridiculous. The world is a sinking ship, and it is sinking because its very structure is rotten. God does not ask the Christian to save the ship, but to save as many of the shipwrecked as he can."[16]

The wave of evil roaring out of a dark sea upon mankind is beyond human power to stop. The best Christians can hope for is avoidance. "Do not attempt to stop it with your weak hand," urged Saint Ignatius Brianchaninov. "Avoid it, protect yourself from it, and that is enough for you. Get to know the spirit of the times, study it so that you can avoid its influence whenever possible."[17]

The duty of Orthodox Christians during the end times is to watch and pray—to be ready when the

Master comes. Only by maintaining vigilance do they stand a chance of recognizing and resisting Antichrist. Only by standing guard through the night do they have a hope of salvation. And those who merely save their own souls in the last days will be doing well. It is recorded that a man came to a Greek elder and asked, "What then is one to do in those times and years?" The elder replied, "Child, in such days as those, he who can save, let him save his own soul, and he shall be called great in the Kingdom of heaven."

God told Ezekiel that when a land sins against Him, the best any one can hope for is to save himself: " 'Even if these three men, Noah, Daniel, and Job, were in it, they would deliver only themselves by their righteousness,' says the Lord GOD" (Ezekiel 14:14).

Finding Sanctuary

For decades and centuries, religious organizations and institutions have been penetrated with a deadening opiate of godlessness which is now reaching its apex. "We see deterioration, ruin, derangement, depersonalization and fading of 'Churchness'," Archimandrite Constantine wrote years ago. "Even Orthodoxy has proven to be ill with the same malady which characterizes Roman Catholicism and Protestantism: infidelity to the Church, reaching to utter disrespectful negligence towards Her and even to the ideological denial of Her original essence."[18]

Saint Ignatius Brianchaninov warned that any hope of reviving Christianity's outer form was futile. "One may recognize the work of the Orthodox faith as approaching its definite conclusion. . . . Do not expect from anyone the restoration of Christianity. The vessels of the Holy Spirit have definitively dried up everywhere, even in the monasteries, those treasuries of piety and grace. . . . The merciful long-suffering of God extends and delays the final end for the small remnant of those who are being saved, while those who are becoming corrupt or have become corrupt attain the fullness of corruption."[19]

Yet the Church of Jesus Christ, even when subjected to institutionalization, is never an institution. "The Church is completely distinct from any kind whatever of organized society on earth," wrote Father Michael Pomazansky.[20] Though all "official" expressions of the church will apostatize, the *Church* will remain pure, offering sanctuary for those souls seeking God.

It has been suggested that the seven churches of Revelation signify seven periods in the life of the whole Church of Christ from its foundation to the end of the world. To the sixth church, Philadelphia, our Lord says, "Because you have kept My command to persevere, I also will keep you from the hour of trial which shall come upon the whole world, to test those who dwell on the earth. Behold, I am coming quickly! Hold fast what you have, that no one may take your crown" (Revelation 3:10, 11).

Based on this understanding, Archbishop Averky explained that "the church of Philadelphia is the next-to-last period in the life of the Church of Christ, the epoch contemporary to us, when the Church will in fact have 'little strength' in contemporary humanity and new persecutions will begin, when patience will be required. . . . By Philadelphia one must understand . . . the Christian Church in general in the last times before the end of the world and the Second Coming of Christ. . . . Especially understandable is the exhortation 'Behold I come quickly. Hold that fast which thou hast, that no man take thy crown.' At that time there will be an increased danger of losing faith because of the multitude of temptations, but thereby the reward for faithfulness will be, so to speak, right at hand, and therefore we must be especially vigilant lest out of lightmindedness we lose the possibility of salvation— as, for example, the wife of Lot lost it."[21]

The Lord promised that His Church would never be defeated, saying that "the gates of Hades shall not prevail against it" (Matthew 16:18). And that those who remain faithful within the Church, especially during the darkness of the last days, will be rescued: "He who endures to the end will be saved" (Matthew 10:22).

Orthodox Christians know that salvation outside the Church is impossible. However, the Church in the end times is destined to become more and more difficult to find. "All the faithful will have to understand that the Church is not there where it appears to be," cautions Alexander Kalomiros. ". . . The Church is where the truth is."[22]

As persecutions mount, the remaining Christians

will hide, and there where they meet to worship God the "Catacomb Church" will exist. Kalomiros continues, "There will always be found a canonical priest, ordained by a canonical bishop, who will follow the Tradition. Around such priests will gather the small groups of the faithful who will remain until the last days. . . . In these small groups the One, Holy, Catholic, and Apostolic Church will be preserved intact."[23]

This Church of "little strength" is not one that many people want to join. Believers will be few, and perhaps far apart. "The Scriptures tell," wrote Saint Ignatius Brianchaninov, ". . . that it is not the majority, but only a very few who travel the narrow path, and in the last days of the world this path will dwindle to the extreme."[24]

Still, while there is yet any light left in the world, any opportunity to serve God openly, Christians should do all they can to communicate the truth. "Walk while you have the light, lest darkness overtake you," admonished our Lord (John 12:35). Eventually there will remain only darkness; then only two possibilities will be open to believers: life within the Catacomb Church or martyrdom. Yet Christ waits at the end of either path.

"It is essential to struggle now against the coming kingdom of darkness, when the possibility of such struggle has not yet been taken from us," wrote Father Boris Molchanoff. "Every avoidance of such struggle now, every compromise with evil, be it even the most insignificant, with the aim of co-existence therewith, permitted today will only increase the difficulty of struggling with it tomorrow."[25]

[1] *The Last Judgement,* p. 175.

[2] *Nihilism,* p. 17.

[3] *Hamlet,* Act III, scene i, line 62.

[4] *Ecumenism, Communism & Apostasy,* pp. 2-3.

[5] *A Ray of Light,* p. 36.

[6] *The Joyful Wisdom,* in *The Complete Works of Friedrich Nietzsche,* p. 168.

[7] *The Brothers Karamazov,* Vol. 2, pp. 763-764.

[8] *The Will to Power,* Vol. II in *The Complete Works of Friedrich Nietzsche,* pp. 50, 101.

[9] "The Blessed Life," Book VII of *Divine Institutes,* as quoted in *Apocalyptic Spirituality,* Bernard McGinn, trans., p. 62.

[10] Eugene (Fr. Seraphim) Rose, "Christian Realism and Worldly Idealism," *The Orthodox Word,* Vol. 22, No. 3 (128), May-June 1986, p. 133.

[11] *The Apocalypse of St. John,* p. 228.

[12] *Orthodox Dogmatic Theology,* p. 344.

[13] *Nihilism,* p. 67.

[14] *Stand Fast in the Truth,* p. 10.

[15] As paraphrased in Miceli, *The Antichrist,* pp. 79-80.

[16] *Against False Union,* p. 25.

[17] Quoted in *Stand Fast in the Truth,* p. 5.

[18] *Ecumenism, Communism & Apostasy,* p. 3.

[19] Quoted by Archimandrite Dimitri in *Myrrhbearers,* Vol. II, No. 3, Autumn 1994, p. 6.

[20] *Orthodox Dogmatic Theology,* p. 224.

[21] *The Apocalypse of St. John,* pp. 76, 71.

[22] *Against False Union,* p. 62.

[23] *Ibid.*

[24] As quoted in Molchanoff, *Antichrist,* p. 27.

[25] *Ibid.,* pp. 27-28.

Chapter 9

The Nature of the Beast

Were . . . a superman to step forward, however, promising an end to all alienation, and love and peace, we may be certain that millions of mortals, indifferent to truth and untruth, would pay him divine homage.

—*Czeslaw Milosz*

Superficially, Antichrist will be like Christ, yet in reality he will be His very antithesis. Appearing to be a god, Antichrist will in fact demonstrate the inverse of godliness: "The coming of the lawless one is according to the working of Satan, with all power, signs, and lying wonders," wrote Saint Paul (2 Thessalonians 2:9).

Satan is the father of lies, as Jesus said, for "there is no truth in him" (John 8:44). As Lucifer's protegé, Antichrist's entire existence will be a monstrous lie which might be stated succinctly as: "Jesus is not God, but I am"; or, as turn-of-the-century Russian mystic Vladimir Soloviev suggested in his "A Short Narrative about Antichrist," "Christ came before me; I appeared next, but that which appears later in time is, in reality,

127

first. I shall come last at the end of history exactly because I am the absolute and final saviour."[1] Saint John the Theologian anticipated this: "Who is a liar but he who denies that Jesus is the Christ? He is antichrist who denies the Father and the Son" (1 John 2:22).

Antichrist will not be Satan incarnate, but a man, for only God has the power to become incarnate in human flesh. Yet he will be thoroughly demon-possessed, allowing Satan to operate freely through him, as Blessed Theodoretus said: "Before Christ's coming there shall appear in the world the enemy of man, the opponent of God, vested in human nature."[2]

Even as a man, Antichrist will possess the most concentrated accumulation of wicked traits possible to human nature. "The Antichrist is to be the Archrebel among men even as Satan is the Archrebel among the angels," wrote Miceli, summarizing the teaching of Saint Irenaeus. "In the Antichrist will be summarized and brought to plenitude all the iniquities and impostures that have taken place from the moment of the fall of the angels, through the fall of man, comprising the evils perpetrated by the generations before Noah and the flood, the evils perpetrated by the perverse generation that crucified Christ, those against His Church right up to and including the flood of crime that will be ushered in by the arrival of the 'man of sin.' In other words the Antichrist will be the culmination and recapitulation of all evils chosen in angelic and human history."[3]

Every aspect of Antichrist's life will serve to copy,

yet mock, God. For example, the lineage of Christ is preserved in the Scripture as an example of holiness nurtured, preserved, and passed along in order to produce the Virgin Mary, who in turn gave birth to God the Word.

The genealogy of Antichrist, on the other hand, will reveal instead the nurturing of generations of vices. Belyaev speculates, "One may assume that innate and acquired evil, accumulating gradually in the long line of Antichrist's forbears, transmitted to each new generation, will ultimately attain the strongest degree which human nature is capable of containing, manifesting and sustaining in the person of Antichrist himself. In him the evil which lives in the human race will reach the apex of its development."[4]

The Ape of God

As Satan has been called *Simia Dei*, or "ape of God," so Antichrist is appropriately labeled *Simia Christi*, or "ape of Christ." Through similitude, they seek to destroy what they imitate. Not only are they personally the reverse of what they seem, but all they affect becomes so.

Christ was born in the Promised Land, but Antichrist, wrote Saint Andrew of Caesarea, "will come from the darkest and most remote lands of the earth, those to which the Devil was banished."[5] Adso of Montier-en-der was more specific: "Just as Our Lord and Redeemer foresaw Bethlehem for himself as the place to assume humanity and to be born for us, so too the devil knew a place fit for that lost man who is called Antichrist, a place from which the root of all evil (1 Tim. 6:10) ought to come, namely, the city of Babylon. Antichrist will be born in that city, which was once a celebrated and glorious pagan center and the capital of the Persian Empire. It says that he will be brought up and protected in the cities of Bethsaida and Corozain, the cities that the Lord reproaches in the Gospel when he says, 'Woe to you, Bethsaida, woe to you, Corozain!' (Matt. 11.21)."[6]

Christ was born of a virgin dedicated to God, but Antichrist "will be born of an evil whore," according to Archimandrite Panteleimon.[7] Christ's Birth, being one of Christendom's major feasts and sources of joy, will be mocked in a particularly odious manner. Commentary exists from many Fathers on this point. "From a defiled virgin shall (the devil's) instrument be born," wrote Saint Ephraim the Syrian. Antichrist "becomes man as the offspring of fornication," wrote Saint John of Damascus in the eighth century.[8]

How could a person of such base breeding come to be highly regarded? Soloviev offers this fictional supposition: "His mother, a person of indulgent conduct, was well known in both hemispheres, but too many different people had good reason to believe themselves his father."[9]

Saint Nilus the Myrrhstreaming revealed posthumously in the early 1800s that Antichrist will be born without man's sowing—through artificial insemination. "Antichrist will be born of an unclean, wanton maid. . . . Every evil of the world, every uncleanness, every sin will be embodied in her. Through her conceiving from secret wantonness, all sins will be combined in a womb of uncleanness and will be brought to life together with the spiritual impoverishment of the world. . . . Conceived from such secret and unnatural wantonness, the offspring will be the container of every evil, as opposed to the way in which Christ was the ideal of every good quality, and His Most Pure Mother was the ideal of womanhood."[10]

The Synaxarion for Meatfare Sunday records: "Antichrist shall come and shall be born, as St. Hippolytus of Rome says, of a polluted woman, a supposed virgin, a Jewess of the tribe of Dan." Both the first and last books of the Bible, Genesis and Revelation, agree that the Antichrist shall emerge from this unfortunate Jewish tribe: "Dan shall be a serpent by the way, a viper by the path" (Genesis 49:17). Among the tribes of Israel which the Book of Revelation declares are sealed by the angels for salvation, only the tribe of Dan is omitted (Revelation 7:4-8).

Thus the son of perdition will copy Christ, but not truly. As a broken mirror reflects only a shattered image, so Antichrist can only be a ghastly parody of the Son of God. "For the deceiver sets to liken himself in all things to the Son of God," wrote Saint Hippolytus. "Christ is a lion, so Antichrist is also a lion; Christ is a king, so Antichrist is also a king. . . . The Saviour came into the world in the circumcision, and he will come in the same manner. The Lord sent apostles among all the nations, and he in like manner will send false apostles. The Saviour gathered the sheep that were scattered abroad, and he in like manner will bring together a people that is scattered abroad. The Lord gave a seal to those who believed in Him, and he will give one in like manner. The Saviour appeared in the form of man, and he too will come in the form of man. The Saviour raised up and showed his holy flesh like a temple, and he will raise a temple of stone in Jerusalem."[11]

But the word "Antichrist" also suggests the exact opposite of Christ, as third-century theologian Origen claimed: "I hold that there exists not only the word Christ, but also the word, the Antichrist; there exists Christ the truth and the Antichrist the counterfeit truth; there is the wisdom that is Christ and the false wisdom that is the Antichrist. . . . We discover all the virtues personified in Christ and all the counterfeit virtues incarnated in the Antichrist."

Life Parallels

Schema-Archimandrite Lavrenty of Chernigov-Trinity Convent, a nineteenth-century Russian monastic, described a scene which perhaps serves as a contrast to the scriptural story of Jesus as a twelve-year-old boy remaining in the temple out of love for His Father: "While still a youth he [Antichrist] will be very capable and smart, especially after he, as a boy of twelve, walking with his mother in the garden, meets satan, who will come from the very depths and enter into him. The boy will shudder with fright, but satan will say: 'Do not be afraid, I will help you.' And this boy will mature into Antichrist in human form."[12]

From that time forward, Satan will never leave Antichrist, for "God, foreknowing the strangeness of the choice that he would make, allows the devil to take up his abode in him," as Saint John of Damascus wrote.[13] The "terrible spirit," as Dostoevsky called Satan, shall penetrate the youth's being, forming in him a fearful plan for world enslavement. He sees he must follow "the clever Spirit, the terrible Spirit of death and destruction, and to such end accept deceit and falsehood and lead people consciously to death and destruction and deceive them moreover all of the way, so that they do not notice whither they are being led, so that at least on the way those pathetic blind creatures shall believe themselves happy."[14]

When Antichrist reaches thirty years, corresponding to the age at which Jesus began his public ministry, he will also begin his public appearance. Antichrist's arrival on the world stage will be an event of great moment. Since he is the false messiah, he will attempt through many signs to replicate the coming of the Son of God on earth.

Antichrist is expected to be a man of great physical beauty, whose countenance may even resemble that of our Lord Jesus Christ. "He will be a man of stupendous talents and spiritual force," wrote contemporary Roman Catholic author Romano Guardini. "... He will also be filled with religious power. Indeed, he will even have a certain resemblance to Christ, for it will be said also of him that he is mortally wounded and yet alive, in other words, that he has sacrificed himself and vanquished, so that there will be something perversely redemptory about him that is directed against the living God and His Christ."[15]

He will appear benevolent and benign, uncommonly good and wise. His clarity of thought, power of persuasion and "sensitivity" to every issue will appeal to a world despairing of many apparently insoluble problems.

"As the Lord showed Himself to the world and brought His activity to perfection as *Prophet, King and High Priest,*" wrote Father Boris Molchanoff, "so Antichrist also will concentrate a threefold authority in his own hands and will carry out his pernicious activity as a *teacher* of all mankind, as the *monarch* of a universal kingdom, and as the *high priest* of all religions, demanding that all worship him as divine."[16]

An Imitation of Christ

But Antichrist's blatant imitation of Christ will not go beyond outward illusions. Inwardly he will be utterly devoid of Christian qualities. Yet few will notice the absence of mercy, love and patience, for, as philosopher Vladimir Soloviev described it, "he will cast a glittering veil of good and righteousness over his secret iniquity."

A mankind accustomed to laser shows, high-definition television and other spectacles will be thrilled by Antichrist. The media will love him; public figures of all types will turn out in his support. Yet the enthusiasm they feel will have sinister origins. Saint Ignatius Brianchaninov warns, "The false spirits, sent throughout the world, will incite in men a generally high opinion of the antichrist, universal ecstasy, irresistible attraction to him."[17]

Antichrist will feign compassion while actually loathing humanity. He will promise to free while planning to enslave. With all his strength he will undertake to complete the work begun by his master through the "mystery of lawlessness." Those who serve him will, by so doing, build their own prisons, voluntarily constructing the chambers in which they will eventually suffer excruciating and unending torments.

Saint Cyril of Jerusalem predicted, "At first indeed he will put on a show of mildness (as though he were a learned and discreet person), and of soberness and benevolence: and by the lying signs and wonders of his magical deceit having beguiled the Jews, as though he were the expected Christ, he shall afterwards be characterized by all kinds of crimes of inhumanity and lawlessness, so as to outdo all unrighteous and ungodly men who have gone before him."[18]

Yet, in spite of all warnings recorded throughout history about this man and the evils he will unleash in the world, few will truly recognize him. He will be viewed as the ultimate success story, a model of achievement inspiring emulation. His ability to meet challenges and overcome obstacles will be shamelessly admired. He himself will be idolized as the "perfect" man, successful in every sphere, a virtual superman of accomplishment. He will become the fantasy hero of men and women alike.

Antichrist's worldly success will make him irresistible to those for whom the world is everything. *Everyone*, even Christians, will feel an urgency to honor him. "The Antichrist must be understood as a spiritual phenomenon," writes Father Seraphim Rose. "Why will everyone in the world want to bow down to him? Obviously, it is because there is something in him which responds to something in us—that something being a lack of Christ in us. If we will bow down to him (God forbid that we do so!), it will be because we will feel an attraction to some kind of external thing, which might even look like Christianity, since 'Antichrist' means the one who is 'in place of Christ' or looks like Christ."[19]

Infernal Royalty

Antichrist will pay homage not to God the Father, but only to the "ruler of this world" (John 16:11), who is also called "ruler of the demons" (Mark 3:22). "He shall honor a god of fortresses," the Prophet Daniel predicted (Daniel 11:38), becoming a "strong man" himself, the supreme prince of this world. Daniel further warned that Antichrist as "royalty" would destroy both the Jews' city, Jerusalem, and their temple: "And the people of the prince who is to come shall destroy the city and the sanctuary" (Daniel 9:26).

It is very instructive to note Niccolo Machiavelli's

sixteenth-century characterization of the definitive worldly prince. This ruthless individual, affecting noble sentiments but exterminating all opposition, bears a striking resemblance to the person of Antichrist: "A prince . . . must not mind incurring the charge of cruelty for the purpose of keeping his subjects united and faithful. . . . It is well to seem merciful, faithful, humane, sincere, religious . . . ; but you must have the mind so disposed that when it is needed to be otherwise you may be able to change to the opposite qualities. [A prince] must have a mind disposed to adapt itself according to the wind . . . to act against faith, against charity, against humanity, and against religion . . . to do evil if constrained. . . . The end justifies the means. Let a prince therefore aim at conquering and maintaining the state, and the means will always be judged honourable and praised by every one, for the vulgar is always taken by appearances and the issue of the event; and the world consists only of the vulgar, and the few who are not vulgar are isolated when the many have a rallying point in the prince."[20]

In his *Three Conversations*, Vladimir Soloviev depicts a prince who meets with a group of Russians on the Mediterranean shore to discuss the problems of the world. This prince does not claim to be a materialist, and longs to secure for the inhabitants of earth peace, justice, and well-being.

During the course of three conversations, an ancient manuscript reveals that a superman will one day arise and accomplish all that the prince hopes for. This superman, as Czech novelist Czeslaw Milosz points out, "considers his vocation the organizing of society so that the commands of the Gospel are implemented. And, let us stress, he does not know he is the Antichrist. He does not suspect it until the moment when he consciously puts himself above Christ because Christ was no more than his predecessor, who died and was not resurrected, whereas he will accomplish that which was proclaimed by his predecessor. This superman believes he acts out of love for man, but in fact he loves only himself. . . . His rule is based upon a lie that must provoke the worst possible effects. . . . The lie is tantamount to demanding that both what is God's and what Caesar's be rendered unto Caesar—a citizen may be happy, but only at the price of complete obedience in all his thoughts and deeds. The disobedience of the Christians is, for Solovyov, a test thanks to which the ruler of genius reveals who he really is."[21]

"666"

Much speculation has gone into this number ever since Saint John the Theologian challenged those with understanding to calculate its meaning: "Here is wisdom. Let him who has understanding calculate the number of the beast, for it is the number of a man: His number is 666" (Revelation 13:18).

Using ancient forms of reckoning which attribute number values to letters in various languages, this number has been associated with many names. Saint Irenaeus calculated "Latinos" and "Titan." Others found the number of the beast in the names of Napoleon and Julian the Apostate, and in the title of the Pope of Rome as Vicar of the Son of God: *Vicarius Filii Dei.* However, these are arbitrary results, and it is unlikely that Saint John had Antichrist's proper name in mind.

Father Sloet, a Catholic priest, determined in the late 1800s that the Hebrew letters for "King of the Jews" are numerically equivalent to 666. This interpretation certainly accords with the traditional understanding that the Antichrist will be accepted by the Jews as their Messiah.

Saint Andrew of Caesarea says the name associated with the number of the beast will only be revealed in the "time of temptation," that is, the last days: "A careful testing of the number, and likewise of everything else written about him [the Antichrist] will be revealed to those who think soundly and are vigilant by the time of temptation."[22]

Saint Irenaeus insists that no one should claim to know with certainty the name, since "danger . . . shall overtake those who falsely presume that they know the name of Antichrist." He points out, however, that the number represents "a summing up of the whole of that apostasy which has taken place during six thousand years."[23]

There is a relationship between the name, the mark, and the image of the beast, and Saint John wrote that "they have no rest day or night, who worship the beast and his image, and whoever receives the mark of his name" (Revelation 14:11). *Epiphany Journal* reported that "in Kabbalistic numerology, with which John was most assuredly familiar, the number six is the sign of complete manifestation; it is the last point before the number seven which is the number of God. Six therefore would represent the kingdom of man and nature without God; carried to the third power (666) it could signify the extension of godlessness into every sphere—body, mind and soul. (The number six, as others have noted, also appears three times in every UPC [Universal Product Code] symbol.)"[24]

But what is the "image" of the beast? Recall that King Nebuchadnezzar had dreamed of a great image—a figure with a gold head, silver chest, bronze belly and iron legs. Daniel had interpreted the king's dream, saying that the different sections and metals of the image represented the four Gentile world empires, of which Babylon was the first.

The image doubtless has a more inclusive meaning—the embodiment of the *kingdom of man* on this earth. For Daniel tells Nebuchadnezzar, "And in the days of these kings the God of heaven will set up a kingdom which shall never be destroyed; and the kingdom shall not be left to other people; it shall break in pieces and consume all these kingdoms, and it shall stand forever" (Daniel 2:44).

This latter, of course, is the Kingdom of God; the stone cut out of the mountain without hands. However, Nebuchadnezzar clearly had ears only for the first part of the prophecy. Soon afterward, he constructed "an image of gold, whose height was sixty cubits and its width six cubits." And then the king "commanded, O peoples, nations, and languages, that at the time you hear the sound of the horn, flute, harp, lyre, and psaltery, in symphony with all kinds of music, you shall fall down and worship the gold image that King Nebuchadnezzar has set up; and whoever does not fall down and worship shall be cast immediately into the midst of a burning fiery furnace" (Daniel 3:1, 4-6).

Saint John the Theologian prophesies a latter-day replay of the image which must be worshiped: "And he deceives those who dwell on the earth . . . telling [them] . . . to make an image to the beast. . . . He was granted power to give breath to the image of the beast, that the image of the beast should both speak and cause as many as would not worship the image of the beast to be killed" (Revelation 13:14, 15).

Saint Irenaeus found in the number of the beast both a connection with previous types of Antichrist and a relationship to the image: "And there is therefore in this beast, when he comes, a recapitulation made of all sorts of iniquity and of every deceit, in order that all apostate power, flowing into and being shut up in him, may be sent into the furnace of fire. Fittingly, therefore, shall his name possess the number six hundred and sixty-six, since he sums up in his own person all the commixture of wickedness which took place previous to the deluge, due to the apostasy of the angels. For Noah was six hundred years old when the deluge came upon the earth, sweeping away the rebellious world, for the sake of that most infamous generation which lived in the times of Noah. And [Antichrist] also sums up every error of devised idols since the flood, together with the slaying of the prophets and the cutting off of the just. For that image which was set up by Nebuchadnezzar had indeed a height of sixty cubits, while the breadth was six cubits; on account of which Ananias, Azarias, and Misael, when they did not worship it, were cast into a furnace of fire, pointing out prophetically, by what happened to them, the wrath against the righteous which shall arise towards the [time of the] end. For that image, taken as a whole, was a prefiguring of this man's coming, decreeing that he should undoubtedly himself alone be worshipped by all men. Thus, then, the six hundred years of Noah, in whose time the deluge occurred because of the apostasy, and the number of the cubits of the image for which these just men were sent into the fiery furnace, do indicate the number of the name of that man in whom is concentrated the whole apostasy of six thousand years, and unrighteousness, and wickedness, and false prophecy, and deception; for which things' sake a cataclysm of fire shall also come [upon the earth]."[25]

Ananias, Azarias, and Misael are better known by their Babylonian names: Shadrach, Meshach and Abednego. Three brave Hebrew lads refused to bow down to Nebuchadnezzar's image, and in consequence of the king's command, were thrown into a furnace of fire. Although the furnace was heated seven times hotter than usual (prefiguring the seven years of the last week?), the boys were seen walking unharmed in the midst of the flames. Not only that, but another person walked with them. Astonished, Nebuchadnezzar cried out: "The form of the fourth is like the Son of God!" (Daniel 3:25).

Shadrach, Meshach and Abednego personify the ageless Church of Christ (though perhaps most particularly the Catacomb Church of the end times) in her struggle against the spirit of Antichrist, for the Lord promised that "where two or three are gathered together in My name, I am there in the midst of them" (Matthew 18:20).

Small wonder that these heroes of truth are remembered every day of the liturgical year, for the seventh song, or *eirmos*, of numerous canons and akathists is reserved as a testimonial to them. This *eirmos* is from the Canon to our Lord Jesus Christ: "When the golden idol was worshiped in the plain of Dura, Thy three children despised the godless order. Thrown into the fire, they were bedewed and sang, Blessed art Thou, O God of our fathers."

Nebuchadnezzar did not command his subjects to worship *him*, but rather the golden image, representing the Kingdom of Man. He wanted to bind the world in its entirety ("O peoples, nations, and languages") to worldliness. Fittingly, this took place in Babylon, which the Book of Revelation calls a whore: "And on her forehead a name was written: MYSTERY, BABYLON THE GREAT, THE MOTHER OF HARLOTS AND OF THE ABOMINATIONS OF THE EARTH" (Revelation 17:5).

Saint Andrew of Caesarea also regards the city of Babylon as being synonymous with the kingdom of man, whose fulfillment will be realized by Antichrist: "We, being guided and forming our conception according to the sequence of events, think that the harlot is in general the earthly kingdom, represented as it were in one body, or the city which is to reign even unto the coming of Antichrist."

The Kingdom of God, on the other hand, is not of this world. As Father Michael Oleksa points out, "Of all the major world religions, Christianity alone affirms the *eternal* significance of the cosmos."[26] Therefore Christians stand alone as the sole judge of, and threat to, worldliness.

Nebuchadnezzar correctly understood that worldliness was a tool of subordination, a means of consolidating and maintaining his power over masses of people. No one could be allowed another point of view, for rejection of the world constituted rejection of him as king of that world!

These same considerations will animate Antichrist to set up his terrible image, which, as Saint John relates, will have "breath" and speak, condemning to death those who refuse to worship it. This will be Nebuchadnezzar's image of the kingdom of man, having attained its most monstrous satanic fulfillment.

---

[1] Paul Marshall Allen, *Vladimir Soloviev, Russian Mystic,* p. 368.

[2] *A Short Exposition of the Divine Dogmas,* as quoted in Molchanoff, *Antichrist,* p. 2.

[3] *The Antichrist,* pp. 52-53.

[4] *On Atheism and Antichrist*, Vol. 1, p. 193, as quoted in Molchanoff, *Antichrist*, p. 2.

[5] *Exegesis on the Eleventh Chapter of the Apocalypse*, ch. 30, as quoted in *ibid.*, p. 2.

[6] *Apocalyptic Spirituality*, Bernard McGinn, trans., p. 91. Adso of Montier-en-der was a noted hagiographer of the tenth century. In 950 he wrote an apocalyptic treatise, based largely on material from compilers (such as Bede) of traditional, patristic sources, for the Frankish Queen Gerberga.

[7] *A Ray of Light*, p. 78.

[8] "An Exact Exposition of the Orthodox Faith," Book IV, ch. XXVI, in *Nicene and Post-Nicene Fathers*, Vol. IX, p. 99.

[9] *Vladimir Soloviev, Russian Mystic*, p. 377.

[10] *A Ray of Light*, p. 76.

[11] "Treatise on Christ and Antichrist," as quoted in Miceli, *The Antichrist*, p. 88.

[12] "The Prophetic Gift," *Orthodox America*, October 1989, p. 6.

[13] "An Exact Exposition of the Orthodox Faith," Book IV, ch. XXVI, in *Nicene and Post-Nicene Fathers*, Vol. IX, p. 99.

[14] *The Brothers Karamazov*, Vol. 1, p. 301.

[15] *The Lord*, p. 510.

[16] *Antichrist*, p. 4.

[17] "On Miracles and Signs," *Orthodox Life*, Vol. 45, No. 2, March-April 1995, p. 38.

[18] "Catechetical Lectures," Lecture XV, part 12, in *Nicene and Post-Nicene Fathers*, Vol. VII, pp. 107-108.

[19] Christensen, *Not of This World*, p. 772.

[20] *The Prince*, pp. 89, 93, 94.

[21] "Science Fiction and the Coming of Antichrist," *Epiphany*, Vol. 6, No. 4, Summer 1986, pp. 82-83.

[22] *Exegesis on the Eleventh Chapter of the Apocalypse*, ch. 37, as quoted in *The Apocalypse of St. John*, p. 149.

[23] "Against Heresies," Book V, ch. 27, in *The Ante-Nicene Fathers*, Vol. I, p. 557.

[24] *Epiphany Journal*, Vol. 4, No. 1, Fall 1983, p. 75.

[25] "Against Heresies," Book V, ch. 29, in *The Ante-Nicene Fathers*, Vol. I, p. 558.

[26] "Icons and the Cosmos," *Epiphany Journal*, Vol. 8, No. 4, Summer 1988, p. 75; emphasis added.

Chapter 10

Why the Devil
Hates a Crowd

The woman who purposely destroys her unborn child is guilty of murder.

—*Saint Basil the Great*

Scientists estimate that in the year 1800, Earth's human population stood at one billion. One hundred thirty years later, in 1930, it had reached two billion, and in 1960 three billion. The United Nations Population Division reported in 1994 that 5.7 billion people inhabited the world and three more were born every second. At the current rate, 90 million more people—a number equivalent to the population of Mexico—will be added every year this decade.[1]

Worldwatch Institute predicts that in the year 2030 the Earth's population may reach 8.9 billion. "Fresh, clean water could be scarce—and prohibitively expensive. The prices of many foods . . . could also skyrocket, with worldwide grain production unable to keep up with the rising human tide. . . . Worldwide fish stocks [could] collapse from overfishing. . . . Pollution could increase dramatically. . . . There could be widespread political instability . . . increased consumption of resources . . . [due to] ominous trends of burgeoning population."[2]

Paul R. Ehrlich, author of *The Population Explosion,* has claimed that fifty-five percent of environmental problems identified since 1850 can be attributed simply to increased population. Those who agree with this assessment pronounce the human upsurge to be life-threatening: "If we don't do something about the population problem, then really the survival of the planet will be at stake," declares Dr. Nafis Sadik, Executive Director of the U.N. Population Fund.[3] Timothy Wirth, U.S. Undersecretary of State for Global Affairs, agrees. "The population problem is a serious one which concerns every person on the planet," he said at Atlanta's Carter Center. "Overpopulation will overwhelm all our political institutions, all our economic institutions. It will destroy the environment around us."[4]

Are these gloomy attitudes justified?

The Holy Scriptures make it clear that the fertility and growth of mankind has resulted from God's blessing and will: "So God created man in His own image; in the image of God He created him; male and female He created them. Then God blessed them, and God said to them, 'Be fruitful and multiply; fill the earth' " (Genesis 1:27, 28).

The Population Threat

Bloated-earth propaganda has been drummed into modern thinking so thoroughly that humanity's numbers are now considered not merely a crisis, but the mother of all crises. One commentator hysterically claimed, "Wars, riots, unemployment, hunger, disease and all the social problems we face daily are due to just one cause—overpopulation. What is the answer? Birth control!"[5]

The Population Crisis Committee, an advocacy group in Washington, warns: "We must stabilize the world's population in the next century, and . . . the only acceptable way to achieve that goal is to give women real choice about childbearing, including very high quality reproductive services."[6]

In actual practice, of course, euphemisms like "birth control" and "reproductive services" primarily mean abortion. Visible corpses are perceived as the best way of insuring that new names are not added to the roster of living humans. Abortion has been loudly touted as a woman's "right" and a prerogative of her "choice," but these emotion-grabbing buzz words serve primarily to draw the gullible into a foray which many would otherwise shun.

Even those who refuse to identify abortion by its most correct name, a sin, must recognize that it is uncivilized, violent, immoral, and contrary to basic human nature. No humane logic can justify the voluntary extermination of living yet unborn infants by their own mothers. Abortion is quite possibly the premier manifestation of social negation in our "post-Christian" times. Consequently, a host of secondary issues have been contrived to, in a sense, sugarcoat this filth and make it palatable.

The energy driving the reproductive rights campaign is by no means the so-called "freedom" or "health" of women. Females who are herded into abortion chambers are treated with greater contempt than common livestock; they are wounded physically, psychically and spiritually, and robbed of a child they will never have a chance to know. Yet because this travesty is presented as something wonderful, women continue to claim their "reproductive rights" and sacrifice their precious offspring to bandits.

Meanwhile, the real reason that abortion is being foisted on nations throughout the world has gone all but unnoticed. Women's liberation is not the goal (quite the contrary!), but something far more insidious: a numbers reduction for all humanity!

A Working Campaign

From the legalization of abortion in 1973 through 1993, more than twenty-eight million babies were aborted in the United States. This is twenty-three times the number of all U.S. soldiers (1.2 million) lost in *all* wars since this country's foundation. It is almost five times the number of Jews massacred in the Nazi Holocaust.

In 1990, Ken Burns' documentary pricked the national conscience over the human cost of the Civil War.

Over 500,000 soldiers died in that conflagration, more Americans than in any other war. Yet during the year in which the documentary's popularity played out, 1.6 million children were legally butchered by abortion in this country alone. Worldwide, that abortion figure was fifty-five million. Across the planet, 105 babies are killed by their mothers every minute.

The U.S. Agency for International Development is working surreptitiously with Planned Parenthood affiliates (such as Brazil's BEMFAM) to coerce Third World nations to reduce live births. A recently declassified government document revealed that "at least a third of all Brazilian women had been sterilized . . . and the procedure was often done without consent."[7] In China and other countries, families face severe penalties for having more than one child, and governmentally forced abortions are not uncommon.

It is a fact that nearly every Western nation has been given the hard-sell on abortion, and the result has been an actual decline in the rate of world population growth. Flushed with success, the United Nations Population Division now predicts that the rate of increase will drop from the present 1.7 percent to one percent by the year 2025. Even lower percentages are hoped for.

Yet many find the so-called "population explosion" to be nothing more than myth, hysteria, and diatribe. In 1983, Thomas Sowell of the Hoover Institution calculated that the entire world's population, then about 4.4 billion, could be housed in typical one-story, single-family homes, four persons to a house with a front and back yard—all in the state of Texas. The authors of *Eco-Sanity* claim that all people alive today "could all stand inside the city limits of Jacksonville, Florida—an area less than 0.03 percent the size of the U.S."[8] Other researchers have examined the economic, environmental and political aspects of this question and concluded that fears associated with "overpopulation" are absolutely groundless.

If so, then one must ask why 150,000 humans are destroyed daily by abortion. If the license of selfish men and women is not the issue, nor the general benefit of Planet Earth, what is? Why is this generation being murdered *en masse?*

The Black Hand

Human sacrifice, frequently requiring the ritualistic dismemberment of children, is quite common in pagan cultures. For instance, a bizarre Indian society once thrived in what is now Mexico. Excavations have unearthed thousands of skulls of people who were ceremonially murdered. Whatever deities this unfortunate tribe believed they worshiped by these acts, they were in fact serving Satan.

Modern man, being technically oriented and "enlightened," considers overt human sacrifice appalling and superstitious. Yet he can easily offer up his children, in numbers (and for reasons) that would surely have bewildered those ancient Indians, on the altars of Convenience, Freedom of Choice, and Personal Fulfillment.

This does not disturb him—he considers his own pleasures paramount.

In rejecting Christ, society has again become pagan, which is to say, demon-worshiping. Human sacrifice has re-emerged, not as a superstitious practice, but as one rife with scientific, economic, and social justifications. On stainless-steel tables, in scrubbed rooms reeking of antiseptic and anesthetic, women offer the fruit of their wombs up to a merciless idol who scorns both them and their costly sacrifice. And this abominable crime is no longer limited to some freak group of deluded savages, but has replicated itself in sinister abandon across the face of the earth.

The voluntary destruction of human babies has become a worldwide epidemic! The enormity of this carnage suggests that a dark intelligence with an ominous design is using abortion to achieve a massive population reduction. "In all of this there can be discerned," wrote Archbishop Averky, "some kind of rationally acting black hand."[9] The black hand which holds the deadly suction tube is guided by an even blacker one.

But why?

Woman with Child

While exiled on Patmos Island in Greece, Saint John the Theologian received a vision: "Now a great sign appeared in heaven: a woman clothed with the sun. . . . Then being with child, she cried out in labor and in pain to give birth" (Revelation 12:1, 2).

Who is this woman? Some have thought her to be the Virgin Mary, but this cannot be. Saint Hippolytus wrote that Saint John "meant most manifestly the Church, endued with the Father's word. . . . The Church [is] always bringing forth Christ, the perfect man-child of God."[10] The woman's child is Christ within His Church. By extension, the child represents all Christians, those whose names are written in the Book of Life.

Saint John's vision continues: "And another sign appeared in heaven: behold, a great, fiery red dragon having seven heads and ten horns, and seven diadems on his heads. His tail drew a third of the stars of heaven and threw them to the earth. And the dragon stood before the woman who was ready to give birth, to devour her Child as soon as it was born" (Revelation 12:3, 4).

The dragon intends to eat this woman's baby. We can understand that the beast wants to destroy Christ and those who belong to Him. But there is also a secondary meaning. An unborn child is at risk.

And who is the dragon? The Scriptures are unequivocal on this point. The dragon is the devil. "And war broke out in heaven: Michael and his angels fought with the dragon; and the dragon and his angels fought, but they did not prevail, nor was a place found for them in heaven any longer. So the great dragon was cast out, that serpent of old, called the Devil and Satan, who deceives the whole world; he was cast to the earth, and his angels were cast out with him" (Revelation 12:7-9).

Isaiah lamented this fall: "How you are fallen from heaven, O Lucifer, son of the morning! . . . For you have said in your heart: '. . . I will exalt my throne above the stars of God. . . . I will be like the Most High' " (Isaiah 14:12-14).

Satan had pridefully set himself above God, so God threw him out of heaven. "Now when the dragon saw that he had been cast to the earth, he persecuted the woman. . . . And the dragon was enraged with the woman, and he went to make war with the rest of her offspring, who keep the commandments of God and have the testimony of Jesus Christ" (Revelation 12:13, 17).

The Fallen Angels

Satan landed on earth with his own angels, all those who had supported his insurrection and had thus themselves become demons. These "stars of heaven" amounted to a third of the original angelic host. How many fallen angels would that be? An extraordinarily large number, for the Prophet Daniel saw in a vision that "a thousand thousands ministered to Him [God]; ten thousand times ten thousand stood before Him" (Daniel 7:10). Saint Cyril of Jerusalem explains that the numbers would certainly be vastly larger, except that "the Prophet could not express more than these."[11]

Fourth-century desert monastic Saint Anthony the Great taught that to replace the fallen angels, God created a new rational creature—man. God placed man in Paradise, which was in a lower heaven and which had previously been under the jurisdiction of the fallen angel.

This accounts for Satan's great hatred of mankind. Saint Ignatius Brianchaninov explains, "So Paradise came under the control of the new creature—man. How very understandable that the new creature became an object of envy and hatred to the fallen angel and his satellites? The reprobate spirits, led by their chief, tried to seduce the newly created men to make them share their fall, and so as to have adherents or associates of the same mind; and they endeavored to infect them with the poison of their hatred for God. In this they succeeded."[12]

Mankind was created specifically to fill the ranks in heaven vacated by the fallen angels, as Saint John of Kronstadt explained: "The Lord deigned to create man out of dust and with such earthly beings to complete the lack in the angelic worlds, which was a consequence of the falling away of the proud spirits. And this was infinite shame and infinite punishment to the proud ones."[13]

Satan's reign as "ruler of this world" (John 14:30) can last only until the Lord returns in glory. God alone knows when that will be, but His commandment to "multiply [and] fill the earth" (Genesis 1:28) offers a clue. As the earth's population increases, conditions are optimized for Christ's Second Coming.

"The world continues," wrote Archimandrite Panteleimon, "because not all who are suitable for the Kingdom of Christ have entered it, or, not as many as are necessary have yet entered. The Lord has said: *And other sheep I have, which are not of this fold: them also I must bring, and they shall hear My voice, and there shall be one fold, and one shepherd* (John 10:16). When all seeking salvation in the true God have done so, then the end will draw near, and the Antichrist will appear."[14]

The world must continue until Christ has fully gathered His children from the ranks of mankind. According to Elder Lavrenty, a nineteenth-century Russian monastic and visionary, "Until the number of fallen angels is restored, the Lord will not come to judge. But in the last time [i.e., at the very end] the Lord will add to the number of angels from those living who are written in the Book of Life, in order to make up the number of the fallen."[15]

Only when there are enough believers to fill the places in heaven vacated by the fallen angels, will Christ return! This explains as nothing else could the satanic inspiration behind population control.

Of course, the devil did not wait until the twentieth century to begin his campaign to reduce the numbers of mankind. Jesus said of Satan, "He was a murderer from the beginning" (John 8:44). Throughout human history Satan has used numerous weapons—war, suicide, disease, to name a few—to kill off his enemy, mankind. Abortion differs from these only in being the most numerically efficacious approach he has yet found.

Our Modern Holy Innocents
This end-times decimation of children was gruesomely prefigured when the Lord first came to earth in

the flesh. In those days the "Holy Innocents," all the babies in Bethlehem younger than two years, died for His sake. Saint Matthew tells the poignant story of those first martyrs, whom Herod murdered in his vain attempt to eradicate the infant Jesus. "A voice was heard in Ramah, lamentation, weeping, and great mourning, Rachel weeping for her children, refusing to be comforted, because they are no more" (Matthew 2:18).

Two thousand years later, innocent babies are again being martyred for Christ. But Satan no longer needs a Herod to do his will. His accomplices now are modern mothers, the "health professionals" who assist them, and the friends, relatives, lovers and husbands who encourage—often nearly coerce—them to consent to the murder of their own children. The voice of Rachel is still heard from many of these women, but now with the added poignancy of bitter remorse for a deed that cannot be undone.

In spite of this widespread and powerful campaign to strip the earth of existing or potential Christians, the Bible reveals that Satan will be frustrated. For when the dragon stood before the pregnant woman, ready to devour her baby when it was born, something quite unexpected happened: "She bore a male Child. . . . And her Child was caught up to God and His throne" (Revelation 12:5).

The term "caught up" appears only three times in the Bible, always describing the experience of humans being lifted into heaven. Believers will be "caught up" once and for all at Christ's Return: "We who are alive and remain until the coming of the Lord will by no means precede those who are asleep. For the Lord Himself will descend from heaven with a shout, with the voice of an archangel, and with the trumpet of God. And the dead in Christ will rise first. Then we who are alive and remain shall be caught up together with them in the clouds to meet the Lord in the air" (1 Thessalonians 4:15-17).

These verses strongly suggest that the demonic murder of babies for the sake of a fallacious "population control" (or any other reason) is itself a sign that the end is near. It is a prelude to Christ's Return, when His elect will be gathered "from the four winds, from one end of heaven to the other" (Matthew 24:31).

The Scriptures reveal that Satan's attempt to keep heaven empty will fail. For, if "God is able to raise up children to Abraham from these stones" (Matthew 3:9), it is certainly within His power to raise up His children, all of them, to Christ. Our Lord leaves weeping Rachel with the consolation that her babies, all those sacrificed for His sake, will be saved. "Thus says the LORD: 'Refrain your voice from weeping, and your eyes from tears; for your work shall be rewarded, says the LORD, and they shall come back from the land of the enemy. There is hope in your future, says the LORD, that your children shall come back to their own border' " (Jeremiah 31:16, 17).

[1] *The Atlanta Journal/Constitution*, May 23, 1992, p. E1.

[2] *The Atlanta Journal/Constitution*, Aug. 28, 1994, p. D1.

[3] *The Atlanta Journal/Constitution*, May 23, 1992, p. E1.

[4] *The Atlanta Journal/Constitution*, Feb. 25, 1994, p. B4.

[5] Martha Pendley, letter to the editor, *The Atlanta Constitution*, July 31, 1992, p. A11.

[6] *The Atlanta Journal/Constitution*, May 23, 1992, p. E1.

[7] "Developing Countries Fight Population Schemes," *Catholic Twin Circle*, Vol. 28, No. 29, July 19, 1992.

[8] As quoted in *The Atlanta Journal/Constitution*, Sept. 15, 1994, p. A13.

[9] *Stand Fast in the Truth*, p. 8.

[10] "Treatise on Christ and Antichrist," in *The Ante-Nicene Fathers*, Vol. V, p. 217.

[11] "Catechetical Lectures," Lecture XV, part 24, in *Nicene and Post-Nicene Fathers*, Vol. VII, p. 112.

[12] *The Arena*, p. 185.

[13] Quoted by Bishop Nektary in "The Mystical Meaning of the Tsar's Martyrdom," *The Orthodox Word*, Vol. 24, Nos. 5-6, Sept.-Dec. 1988, p. 315.

[14] *A Ray of Light*, p. 37.

[15] "The Prophetic Gift," *Orthodox America*, October 1989, p. 6.

Chapter 11

The Seven-Year Reign
of Antichrist

By no joy sated, filled by no success,
Still whoring after shapes that flutter past,
This last ill moment of sheer emptiness—
The poor man yearns to hold it fast . . .
                              —Goethe, "Faust"

In 606 B.C., Nebuchadnezzar conquered Jerusalem. The Second Book of Chronicles records that his soldiers "burned the house of God, broke down the wall of Jerusalem, burned all its palaces with fire, and destroyed all its precious possessions" (2 Chronicles 36:19). When the king returned to Babylon, he took with him many Jewish captives, among whom was the Prophet Daniel. It was Daniel who subsequently interpreted Nebuchadnezzar's dream of a giant human figure made of various metals, as discussed in Chapter 3.

The Prophet Jeremiah, who was Daniel's contemporary, had remained in Jerusalem under the Babylonian occupying army. Witnessing the destruction of the

Holy City, Jeremiah prophesied, "This whole land shall be a desolation and an astonishment, and these nations shall serve the king of Babylon seventy years" (Jeremiah 25:11).

Daniel was aware of Jeremiah's prophecy, and when the seventy years were nearly completed, he prayed God would reveal what was to become of his people. In response, God sent the Archangel Gabriel to give Daniel "skill to understand" future history.

"Seventy weeks are determined for your people and for your holy city," Gabriel told Daniel, "to finish the transgression, to make an end of sins, to make reconciliation for iniquity, to bring in everlasting righteousness, to seal up vision and prophecy, and to anoint the Most Holy. Know therefore and understand, that from the going forth of the command to restore and build Jerusalem until Messiah the Prince, there shall be seven weeks and sixty-two weeks; the street shall be built again, and the wall, even in troublesome times. And after the sixty-two weeks Messiah shall be cut off, but not for Himself" (Daniel 9:22-26).

Seventy Weeks

God revealed to Daniel that the history of the world was to be completed over the course of "seventy weeks." Everything necessary "to make an end of sins" and "to bring in everlasting righteousness" was to take place during that period, culminating with the anointing of the Most Holy at our Lord's Second Coming.

It must be understood, however, that Gabriel's

"week" consists of years, not days. One week equals seven years. Seventy weeks of seven equal 490 years, suggesting our Lord's count of how many times Christians are to forgive those who sin against them: "I do not say to you, up to seven times, but up to seventy times seven" (Matthew 18:22).

This seventy-week period began with "the command to restore and build Jerusalem." According to Nehemiah 2:1, King Artaxerxes gave the command to rebuild Jerusalem "in the month of Nisan, in the twentieth year of King Artaxerxes." Many competent authorities, including the Royal Observatory in Greenwich, England, have computed this date to be March 14, 445 B.C.

From the commandment to rebuild Jerusalem, "seven weeks and sixty-two weeks" were to elapse. After this "Messiah shall be cut off." Seven "weeks" plus sixty-two "weeks" equals sixty-nine "weeks," or 483 years. In 1895, Sir Robert Anderson of Scotland Yard calculated that, based on the Jewish lunar/solar year of 360 days, 483 years equaled 173,880 days. He counted 173,880 days from March 14, 445 B.C., and arrived at April 6, A.D. 32.

What is the significance of this date?

Saint Luke wrote that "in the fifteenth year of the reign of Tiberius Caesar, Pontius Pilate being governor of Judea . . . the word of God came to John the son of Zacharias in the wilderness. And he went into all the region around the Jordan, preaching a baptism of repentance for the remission of sins, as it is written in the book of the words of Isaiah the prophet, saying: 'The voice of one crying in the wilderness: "Prepare the way of the LORD" ' " (Luke 3:1-4).

Historical documents confirm that the coronation of Tiberius Caesar as Emperor took place August 19, A.D. 14, following the death of Augustus Caesar. The fifteenth year of Tiberius' reign must therefore have begun on August 19, A.D. 28.

Concerning the days of Saint John the Baptist's preaching, Saint Mark relates, "It came to pass in those days that Jesus came from Nazareth of Galilee, and was baptized by John in the Jordan. And immediately, coming up from the water, He saw the heavens parting and the Spirit descending upon Him like a dove. . . . Now after John was put in prison, Jesus came to Galilee, preaching the gospel of the kingdom of God" (Mark 1:9, 10, 14). Based on the Gospel record, it is possible to assume that our Lord's public ministry began in the fall of the year A.D. 28.

Six months later, during the Passover Feast in the temple, the Jews demanded a sign from Jesus. He replied: " 'Destroy this temple, and in three days I will raise it up.' Then the Jews said, 'It has taken forty-six years to build this temple, and will You raise it up in three days?' " (John 2:19, 20).

This episode further suggests that our Lord's ministry began in A.D. 28, as Grant Jeffrey explains: "The historical records of that time, including Flavius Josephus in his *War of the Jews* tell us that Herod the Great began the restoration of the Temple in 18 B.C. The year of

Christ's first Passover of His public ministry, A.D. 29 is *exactly 46 years* from the commencement of Herod's restoration program in 18 B.C. (Note: only one year exists between 1 B.C. and A.D. 1)."[1]

By Saint John's reckoning, Jesus attended at least three Passovers and was crucified during the fourth, so his public ministry lasted about three and a half years. Therefore, it was on the tenth of the Jewish month of Nisan in the year A.D. 32 that Jesus Christ made His Triumphal Entry into Jerusalem, riding on a colt.

The tenth of Nisan, A.D. 32, corresponds to April 6, A.D. 32, precisely 173,880 days from the day "the command to restore and build Jerusalem" was given! This was a fateful day of decision for the Jewish nation. The Promise of the ages, the very Messiah, approached meekly, with only palm-bearing children and ragtag disciples to cheer Him on. The moment, like their God, came in humility. And though both had been announced, the Jews did not recognize either— because their backs were turned: "But when the chief priests and scribes saw the wonderful things that He did, and the children crying out in the temple and saying, 'Hosanna to the son of David!' they were indignant" (Matthew 21:15).

Luke records that when Jesus saw the city, He "wept over it, saying, 'If you had known, even you, especially in this your day, the things that make for your peace! But now they are hidden from your eyes . . . because you did not know the time of your visitation' " (Luke 19:41-44).

Why were the things that made for their peace hidden? Because on the day of their Savior's lowly entry into the holy city, the Jewish leaders did not recognize the time of their visitation. Not expecting Christ, they rejected Him. They "cut off" their own Messiah! Thus, the sixty-nine weeks previously revealed by God through the Archangel Gabriel were completed.

Between Sixty-nine and Seventy

"With the Lord one day is as a thousand years, and a thousand years as one day," wrote Saint Peter (2 Peter 3:8). Though it seems strange to human reckoning, God placed a great chasm of time between the fulfillment of week sixty-nine and the beginning of week seventy. This interval, often referred to as the Church age, was a gift to believers—to those who, as Saint John wrote, "lived and reigned with Christ for a thousand years" (Revelation 20:4).

Throughout the Church age, Christianity spread through the Gentile world, "the nations," as it is called in the Scriptures. In order for this to be accomplished, Satan had to be bound, so an angel "cast him into the bottomless pit, and shut him up, and set a seal on him, so that he should deceive the nations no more till the thousand years were finished" (Revelation 20:3).

For a (figurative) millennium, the devil lay bound by the Christian monarchy and the Church of Christ grew. While the Gospel was preached throughout the world, Satan continued to be operative, but only (in comparison with his full strength) weakly and secretively, as the "mystery of lawlessness." Yet even so, he labored to prepare for his darling's coming reign of terror.

The Last Week

The Scriptures offer the consolation that Antichrist's "public ministry" will be brief. "Woe to the inhabitants of the earth and the sea! For the devil has come down to you, having great wrath, because he knows that he has a short time" (Revelation 12:12).

Satan knows that Christ will ultimately triumph and that his own demise is foreordained. But he doesn't care, for he is utterly incorrigible. And he knows that, though his period of absolute power will be short, it will nevertheless be long enough to ensnare many people.

The only unknown, apparently, is who among mankind will choose good, and who will choose evil. Man, after all, has free will. Because of this free will, each person can and must "choose . . . this day whom you will serve" (Joshua 24:15).

The "last week" represents the culmination and fulfillment of all world history. At this time the rejection of Christ which originated with God's "chosen people" will reach its demonic nadir. The forces which have clandestinely conspired to defraud God will emerge visibly, horribly, struggling to rend the earth from its divinely placed orbit.

But when does this last week begin? Gabriel gave Daniel two clues to that final seven-year span. Two climactic events will take place—one at the beginning and one in the middle of the week. By observing them, it is possible to discuss the week in terms of two halves. These two halves are quite different from each other.

The First Half Week

"Then he shall confirm a covenant with many for one week," Gabriel said (Daniel 9:27), describing the event which will begin the first half week. "He" refers to "the prince who is to come" of the previous verse, and can be none other than Antichrist. Antichrist will consolidate his power by entering into covenant relationships with many individuals and groups, offering them favors in order to gain their support. But in particular, since Daniel's original question regarded the future of his people, it is expected that Antichrist will make a covenant with the Jews, possibly offering them assurance of military and political protection.

These "rulers of Jerusalem," recognizing the immense power of Antichrist and suspecting the danger of opposing him, will seek this covenant in self-defense. Isaiah rightly describes their agreement as being with "death" himself. "Therefore hear the word of the LORD, you scornful men, who rule this people who are in Jerusalem, because you have said, 'We have made a covenant with death, and with Sheol we are in agreement. When the overflowing scourge passes through, it will not come to us' " (Isaiah 28:14, 15). But God will have the last word, for He replies, "Your covenant with death will be annulled, and your agreement with Sheol will not stand; when the overflowing scourge passes through, then you will be trampled down by it" (Isaiah 28:18).

The first half week, consisting of three and one-half years, will be delineated by the extraordinary ministry of Enoch and Elias: "And I will give power to my two witnesses, and they will prophesy one thousand two hundred and sixty days [three and a half years], clothed in sackcloth" (Revelation 11:3).

The apocryphal Gospel of Nicodemus records a fascinating conversation said to have occurred when Christ harrowed hell and delivered Adam from Hades. On his way to Paradise, Adam met two old men and asked them, "Who are you, who have not seen death, and have not come down into Hades, but who dwell in paradise in your bodies and your souls? One of them answered, and said: I am Enoch, who was well-pleasing to God, and who was translated hither by Him; and this is Helias the Thesbite; and we are also to live until the end of the world; and then we are to be sent by God to withstand Antichrist, and to be slain by him, and after three days to rise again, and to be snatched up in clouds to meet the Lord."[2]

The first half week will end with the murder of Enoch and Elias. Once these witnesses for God's truth are gone, Antichrist will exercise unlimited power, bringing to dark fruition all the demonic dreams of the centuries. "And he was given a mouth speaking great things and blasphemies, and he was given authority to continue for forty-two months [three and a half years]" (Revelation 13:5).

The Second Half Week

Being a deceiver, Antichrist will not honor his agreement with the Jews. He will fiercely turn against those who looked to him for protection: "He has put forth his hands against those who were at peace with him; he has broken his covenant" (Psalm 55:20).

The breaking of the covenant will be followed by a monstrous sacrilege—Antichrist will force the Jews to stop worshiping God with "sacrifice and offering," and will at the same time proclaim *himself* god! "In the middle of the week he shall bring an end to sacrifice and offering, and on the wing of abominations shall be one who makes desolate, even until the consummation" (Daniel 9:27).

This is the abomination which Jesus warned of—a man posing as divinity in the "holy place" of the Lord's House: " 'Therefore when you see the "abomination of desolation," spoken of by Daniel the prophet, standing in the holy place' (whoever reads, let him understand)" (Matthew 24:15).

The desolation of the temple will thus mark the midpoint of Antichrist's seven-year reign. "And from the time that the daily sacrifice is taken away, and the abomination of desolation is set up, there shall be one thousand two hundred and ninety days [three and a half years plus thirty days]" (Daniel 12:11).

The second half week is to be the most difficult time that humanity has ever experienced. All possible negativity and godlessness will deluge the earth, destroying people spiritually and physically. Our Lord spoke of the unmitigated horror of this period when He said, "For then there will be great tribulation, such as has not been since the beginning of the world until this time, no, nor ever shall be" (Matthew 24:21).

That Christians will be under attack for the three and a half years of the Great Tribulation is indicated by the following passage: "But leave out the court which is outside the temple, and do not measure it, for it has been given to the Gentiles. And they will tread the holy city underfoot for forty-two months" (Revelation 11:2). Archbishop Averky explained this cryptic verse thus: "The treading underfoot of the Holy City, Jerusalem, or the ecumenical Church for the course of forty-two months signifies that at the coming of antichrist the faithful will be persecuted for the course of three and a half years."[3]

A Time and Times and Half a Time

"A time and times and half a time" is another scriptural code for three and a half years, as Saint Cyril explains: "*A time* is the one year in which his coming shall for a while have increase; and *the times* are the remaining two years of iniquity, making up the sum of the three years; and *the half a time* is the six months."[4] Daniel writes, "He shall speak pompous words against the Most High, shall persecute the saints of the Most High, and shall intend to change times and law. Then the saints shall be given into his hand for a time and times and half a time" (Daniel 7:25).

No earthly structure can resist Antichrist's infernal

strength and cleverness. Every social, political and economic institution will belong to him; every religious organization will swear allegiance. He will gain absolute control of this world in seven years, and then his reign will suddenly end. "Then I heard the man clothed in linen, who . . . swore by Him who lives forever, that it shall be for a time, times, and half a time; and when the power of the holy people has been completely shattered, all these things shall be finished" (Daniel 12:7).

Yet even this comparatively short span will see the worst bloodbath of terror and torment that the world has ever known. God in His mercy will keep the period brief, otherwise no one would survive: "And unless those days were shortened, no flesh would be saved; but for the elect's sake those days will be shortened" (Matthew 24:22).

For those few who live through the Great Tribulation without having submitted themselves to Antichrist, the greatest sight is in store—the Return of Christ in glory! And those who have died in the Lord will also be awakened to witness this most wonderful of all moments.

Saint Ephraim the Syrian writes, "When three and a half years of the rule and deeds of the foul one will have been fulfilled, and all the temptations of the earth will have been completed, then, as foretold, the Lord will finally appear, like lightning flashing in the sky, the holy, most-pure, terrifying, and glorious God of all, with incomparable glory. Preceding His great glory will be hosts of angels and archangels, all of them like fiery flames; and the river full of terrible boiling fire; Cherubim with downcast eyes and Seraphim flying and covering their faces with fiery wings and with trepidation calling out: 'Arise, you who have died, it is the Bridegroom Who cometh!' "[5]

The Coming of the Thief

Given the scripturally defined duration of the world's "last week," it might appear that calculating the time of Christ's Return is elementary. Once the Great Tribulation has begun, one need only watch for the specified events, then count down three and one-half years from the defiling of the Jewish temple. Even the Antichrist, presumably, will be mindful of his "forty-two months," and expect to battle the Lord only on the last day of the last month.

This simple forecast is untrustworthy, however, since it ignores Jesus' assurance that "of that day and hour no one knows, not even the angels of heaven, but My Father only" (Matthew 24:36). Even Satan, himself a fallen angel, cannot know for sure when the Lord will return. No doubt this contributes to his "great wrath."

God, being sovereign, controls the timing of everything: "It is not for you to know times or seasons which the Father has put in His own authority" (Acts 1:7). The seven years of Daniel's week may therefore ultimately be vastly shorter or longer than chronological years.

It is a curiosity of the divine economy that Jesus often portrayed Himself as a thief. Referring to His Resurrection (see Chapter 5), He spoke of Satan as the master of mankind's "house" thus: "If the master of the house had known what hour the thief would come, he would have watched and not allowed his house to be broken into" (Matthew 24:43).

On the night of His betrayal, the Lord demanded of His captors, "Have you come out, as against a robber, with swords and clubs to take Me?" (Mark 14:48). Following this He was condemned as a lawbreaker and hung among thieves: "Then two robbers were crucified with Him, one on the right and another on the left" (Matthew 27:38).

Both major milestones of sacred history, the Resurrection and the Return, are characterized by this image of a thief. The "day of the Lord" refers, of course, to all the events associated with Christ's Return and Last Judgment. "For you yourselves know perfectly that the day of the Lord so comes as a thief in the night," Saint Paul reminded the Greeks (1 Thessalonians 5:2). Saint Peter also stressed that "the day of the Lord will come as a thief in the night" (2 Peter 3:10).

A thief is one who enters unseen to steal away valuables. The Lord declares that, in spite of all the prophetic utterances of Holy Scripture and the dramatic testimony of unfolding world events, His Return shall nevertheless be *both undetected and unexpected!* "Behold, I am coming as a thief. Blessed is he who watches" (Revelation 16:15).

No one will realize Christ is coming until He has arrived! No one, that is, except those faithful Christians who have been keeping watch. It could well be argued that it is for the sake of these faithful few that all of the prophecies concerning the end times are preserved in Scripture. For they alone will heed them.

The last Christians will be waiting and watching. They will be ready. And they alone among all humanity will perceive the Lord not as a thief, but as the long-awaited Savior! "Therefore if you will not watch, I will come upon you as a thief, and you will not know what hour I will come upon you" (Revelation 3:3).

[1] *Armageddon: Appointment with Destiny,* p. 245.
[2] "The Gospel of Nicodemus," ch. 9, in *The Ante-Nicene Fathers,* Vol. VIII, p. 437.
[3] *The Apocalypse of St. John,* p. 127.
[4] "Catechetical Lectures," Lecture XV, part 16, in *Nicene and Post-Nicene Fathers,* Vol. VII, p. 109.
[5] *A Ray of Light,* Archimandrite Panteleimon, comp., p. 96.

Chapter 12

The First Half Week: World Deception

He will drag every man after himself and drive
innumerable men before himself.
—Saint Gregory the Great

The first recorded act of Satan in the Scriptures is the deception of Adam and Eve. God had filled Adam with wisdom, as Saint Seraphim of Sarov (d. 1833) taught: "Adam was made so wise by this breath of life which was breathed into his face from the creative lips of God, the Creator and Ruler of all, that there never has been a man on earth wiser or more intelligent than he, and it is hardly likely that there ever will be."[1]

Eve, the mother of humanity, was certainly not stupid. If Adam was the wisest man, then his helpmate surely shared his discernment. And yet, they were both taken in by the serpent, who "was more cunning than any beast of the field which the LORD God had made" (Genesis 3:1).

Jesus, of course, was well acquainted with Satan, having been tempted by him in the wilderness. The

Lord called him "a liar" and said, "there is no truth in him" (John 8:44). Having no truth in him means that Satan does not merely lie on occasion or when convenient; he cannot do anything *but* lie!

"How you are fallen from heaven, O Lucifer," lamented the Prophet Isaiah (Isaiah 14:12). Lucifer had ranked first among all created beings in glory and intelligence. And although he was cast out of heaven and his glory darkened, no mortal can hope to match his cleverness.

Since deception is Satan's hallmark, this vice will naturally also characterize his human protegé, Antichrist. "For the father of falsehood will make a show of the works of falsehood," wrote Saint Cyril of Jerusalem, "that the multitudes may think that they see a dead man raised, who is not raised, and lame men walking, and blind men seeing, when the cure has not been wrought."[2]

He will appear to duplicate the miracles which Jesus Christ performed, as Saint Ephraim the Syrian warned: "He will captivate the world with his magical illusions. [A] hill rising from the depths of a great sea, in the form of a large island, will be commanded to leave its place and move to a dry spot on the pleasant shore, to please the onlookers. Although the island will not move from the sea at all, it will appear to be a mountain standing on the shore. . . . In like manner he will step out into the deep and walk on it as if on land, presenting this as an illusion, and many will believe, and praise him, as a powerful god."[3]

The Scriptures teach that Jesus Christ is Truth incarnate, "the way, the truth, and the life" (John 14:6). As the living inversion of Christ, Satan could be called "the false path, the lie, and the death." Antichrist is also referred to as "death" (Isaiah 28:15), as noted in Chapter 11.

The Willing Suspension of Disbelief

Saint Paul explained that many will be vulnerable to Antichrist's deception because they have already rejected Truth. They will believe his lies, because they are already living the Lie. "And then the lawless one will be revealed, whom the Lord will consume with the breath of His mouth and destroy with the brightness of His coming. The coming of the lawless one is according to the working of Satan, with all power, signs, and lying wonders, and with all unrighteous deception among those who perish, because they did not receive the love of the truth, that they might be saved. And for this reason God will send them strong delusion, that they should believe the lie" (2 Thessalonians 2:8-11).

In his "Advent Sermons on Antichrist" written in the nineteenth century, English churchman John Henry Newman wrote of the temptations with which Antichrist will deluge humanity: "He offers baits to tempt men: he promises liberty, equality, trade and wealth, remission of taxes, reforms. He tempts men to rail against their rulers and superiors in imitation of his own revolution. He promises illumination, knowledge, science, philosophy, enlargement of mind. He scoffs at times gone by, at sacred traditions, at every institution which reveres them. He bids man mount aloft, to become a god. He laughs and jokes with men, gets intimate with them, takes their hands, gets his fingers between theirs, grasps them and then they are his."[4]

Antichrist will employ many tools of deceit, but his fundamental deception will be to imitate Jesus Christ. *Simia Christi* will enthrall the world precisely because of his semblance to God the Word. And yet, it is by this that Christians are to discern the impostor's true identity. "Take heed that no one deceives you," our Lord warned. "For many will come in My name, saying, 'I am He,' and will deceive many" (Mark 13:5, 6).

Those whose understanding of God is a materialistic one, who expect Christ to act in certain predictable ways—these will be (and have always been) especially open to satanic manipulation. The Pharisees had expected their Messiah to rescue them from the power of Rome and to establish for himself an earthly kingdom. Because Jesus did not do these things, those Jews could not see in Him their long-awaited Savior.

However, Antichrist *will* build the earthly kingdom the Jews have wanted so long. As Saint Hippolytus says, "None other than Antichrist . . . is . . . to raise the kingdom of the Jews."[5] It is this materialistic view of God and the craving for an earthly kingdom which will render them vulnerable to his deceptions.

Only those who are "not of this world" have a hope of recognizing and resisting the evil one. Their knowledge of the prophecies concerning him, along with a firm foothold in the world to come, will preserve them.

Have I Got a Deal for You!

The world will be completely in Antichrist's thrall, according to Saint John Maximovitch: "Fascinating, intelligent, kind, he [Antichrist] will be merciful—he will act with mercy and goodness; but not for the sake of mercy and goodness, but for the strengthening of his authority. And when he will have strengthened it to the point where the whole world acknowledges him, then he will reveal his face.

"For his capital he will choose Jerusalem, because it was here that the Saviour revealed His Divine teaching and His person. . . . He will do what is pleasing to all—on the condition of being recognized as Supreme Authority. He will allow the Church to exist, will permit her Divine Services, will promise to build magnificent churches, on condition that all recognize him as 'Supreme Being' and worship him. . . .

"Under Antichrist there will be an immense falling away from the faith. Many bishops will change in faith and in justification will point to the brilliant situation of the Church. The search for compromise will be the characteristic disposition of men. Straightforwardness of confession will disappear."[6]

Antichrist will develop a reputation as a phenomenal problem-solver. His uncanny ability to anticipate outcomes and to propose solutions will seem prophetic and visionary to a world unaware of his secret manipulations. War, economic disturbance, social injustice, political instability, religious intolerance—no difficulty will escape his soothing touch.

A cry will rise up (a cry initiated by his own servants) that Antichrist be given more authority—and eventually, all authority. Saint Hippolytus wrote that "when the peoples and tribes see so great virtues and so great powers in him, they will all with one mind meet together to make him king."[7]

Yet, even while he is feigning love for humanity, Antichrist will surreptitiously destroy whatever is left of overtly Christian society in the world. He will remove honest people from positions of power and replace them with his cronies. Only those who are one with him and his methods will prosper. Corruption will fill every realm of society. "His power shall be mighty, but not by his own power; he shall destroy fearfully, and shall prosper and thrive; he shall destroy the mighty, and also the holy people. Through his cunning he shall cause deceit to prosper under his rule; and he shall exalt himself in his heart. He shall destroy many in their prosperity" (Daniel 8:24, 25).

One World Government

The elevation of Antichrist to the position of world leader will correspond to the political development of a unified world government. This concept has been the apple of many a liberal/socialist eye, but only under Antichrist will it become a reality, with all its horrifying implications.

Communism has prepared the way for a unified government, in spite of its failure to complete the Revolution on its own limited terms. But a unified world government must be cemented by something stronger than politics, or even economics. Communism *per se* failed precisely because it lacked a spiritual dimension by which to inspire sacrifice and mutual effort. Under Antichrist a spirituality will be developed which will be similar to Christianity in many outward ways—but it will be Antichristianity.

Examples of the "new spirituality" can already be found in organs of the coming unified world government, such as the United Nations. "But in order to supply people with a 'spiritual' basis for one world government, there has to be something higher: and in the ideas of the United Nations, for example, we see something that looks like a spiritual answer," taught Father Seraphim Rose. "The U.N. claims to be for the foundation of one world government which will not be a tyranny, not based upon any particular idea like Communism, but on something very vague, with no Christian basis for it. In fact, about twenty years ago they built a meditation chapel in the U.N. building, and at that time they had a big discussion about what would be the object of worship in it. You can't have a Cross, because then you're immediately branded as Christian; you can't have anything Moslem or Hindu because again you're identified; it has to be above all religions. Finally they decided on a black stone block. People experience an awesome feeling before it, as before an idol: a very vague kind of religious interest."[8]

The False Prophet

As John the Baptist, "the Forerunner," prepared the way for Jesus' public ministry, a uniquely cunning man will set the stage for Antichrist's advent. This person, referred to in Scripture as "the false prophet," will enthrall the world by means of compellingly staged spectacles.

The purpose of these performances will be to bring more people into Antichrist's camp. "The forerunner of the apostate—the false christ—will perform everything through sorcery and deceit for the deception of men," wrote Saint Andrew of Caesarea, "so that antichrist might be considered as God, being the glorious performer of such miracles and worthy of undoubted glory, like St. John the Baptist who brought believers to the Saviour."

Saint John the Theologian referred to the false prophet as a "beast" whose job is to persuade the masses of Antichrist's spiritual stature. "Then I saw another beast coming up out of the earth, and he had two horns like a lamb and spoke like a dragon. And he exercises all the authority of the first beast in his presence, and causes the earth and those who dwell in it to worship the first beast. . . . He performs great signs, so that he even makes fire come down from heaven on the earth in the sight of men. And he deceives those who dwell on the earth by those signs which he was granted to do in the sight of the beast, telling those who dwell on the earth to make an image to the beast" (Revelation 13:11-14).

Like his chief, the false prophet will be a master of deception. Were it not for Christ's protection, he would in fact deceive all. "For . . . false prophets will rise and show great signs and wonders to deceive, if possible, even the elect" (Matthew 24:24).

A humanity taught by science that whatever they want they can have, and by Hollywood to believe that whatever they see is true, will be enchanted and mystified by the wonders of the false prophet. His magical presentations will pique, and at the same time deaden, the longing in their souls for true heavenly visions.

Although Christ worked many miracles, He refused, in Dostoevsky's words, to "enslave man by a miracle." The Lord would not "perform" for His brethren in Nazareth, for He wanted their faith to be given freely, not induced by magic. He would not display His power to Herod or descend from the Cross on demand.

But enslavement by miracles is what fallen man has always wanted, and what the Antichrist will arrange. "Is the nature of men such," asked Dostoevsky's Grand Inquisitor, "that they can reject miracle, and at the great moments of their life, the moments of their deepest, most agonizing spiritual difficulties, cling only to the free verdict of the heart? . . . And as man cannot bear to be without the miraculous, he will create new miracles of his own for himself, and will worship deeds of sorcery and witchcraft."[9]

People will not look for a deeper significance in the false prophet's exhibitions. They will consider their emotionally charged feelings to be proof, not only of the "truth" which they are witnessing, but of their own cleverness and spiritual discernment. "People will not realize that his miracles do not have any blessed, reasonable goal, no definite meaning, that they are alien to truth, play-acting deprived of meaning, filled with lies, that they are monstrous, malicious, and meaningless, straining to astonish, deceive and entice by the enchantment of a lavish, empty, silly effect," wrote Saint Ignatius Brianchaninov. ". . . All men, led by the light of fallen nature, alienated from the guidance of God's Light, will be enticed into submission to the seducer."[10]

A Sign from Above

The last thing the Pharisees demanded as they watched Christ on the Cross was a sign. "He trusted in God; let Him deliver Him now if He will have Him," they taunted (Matthew 27:43).

Although Jesus refused to satisfy the Jews' morbid curiosity, Antichrist will have no such scruples: "What Christ refused to do will be done by Antichrist," wrote Saint Ephraim the Syrian.

"He will make the lame walk," testifies the Apocalypse of Elijah concerning Antichrist. "He will make the deaf hear. He will make the dumb speak. He will make the blind see. Lepers he will heal. The sick he will cure. The demon-possessed he will exorcize. He will do the things which the Christ did, with the sole exception of raising the dead. By this you will know that he is the lawless one: he has no power to give souls."[11]

"He will give a 'sign from the heavens,' i.e., a sign from the air, the principal domain of Satan," continued Saint Ephraim. Because Satan is the "prince of the power of the air" (Ephesians 2:2), his apparent wonders will take place in this realm. Saint Ignatius Brianchaninov echoed this in the nineteenth century: "The signs of the antichrist will be primarily in the air for it is in this realm that Satan mainly rules."[12]

For this reason the Holy Fathers have counseled Christians to avoid looking curiously into the sky. Though this may seem a strange admonition, it certainly makes sense in the light of the demonic wonders which the false prophet is to work there. "One ought to gaze at the heavens very rarely," warned Saint Symeon the New Theologian (d. 1022) in *The Philokalia,* "for fear of the evil spirits of the air who cause many and divers deceptions in the air."

Schema-Archimandrite Lavrenty maintained that the Jesus Prayer (see pp. 227-228) will be instrumental in shielding Christians from Antichrist's false signs: "In those days there will still be strong warriors, Orthodox pillars, who will be under the powerful influence of the Jesus Prayer. The Lord will cover them with His almighty grace, and they will not see those false signs which will be prepared for all people."[13]

Leading Religious Revival

Exploiting the false spirituality of "New Age" thinking and notions such as the "transcendental unity of religions," Antichrist will pose as a dispenser of wisdom. "He will boast loudly about himself, as his forerunners and his prototypes did, he will call himself a preacher and restorer of the true knowledge of God," wrote Saint Ignatius Brianchaninov. "The non-discerning Christians will see in him a representative and a supporter of true religion and will thus join him. He will proclaim and call himself the promised Messiah, and the children of carnal wisdom will rush to meet him, proclaim his glory, power, and genius,—will proclaim him a god, become his supporters."[14]

Antichrist will produce a doctrine which appears to meet the spiritual needs of all people, regardless of outward religious affiliations. Universalist creeds have in fact already been adopted by many groups, for whom Antichrist will merely supply the missing weight of recognized authority.

Even some Christians will find Antichrist's doctrine palatable, devoid of the "problems" which have made the Holy Scriptures abhorrent to modern man. The institutional churches will abandon God. A great "spiritual revival" will take place, but it will not be the Holy Spirit which is revived. Many will be swept up in the elation and high emotions of this revival, and believe themselves to be spiritually renewed, when they have in fact been defiled.

The False Messiah

Antichrist will aspire not only to total secular power, but to total spiritual power as well. The Jews, who for two thousand years have denied their own Messiah, will find that Antichrist is everything they had wanted Jesus to be. A prayer in the *Lenten Triodion* reads, "Compelled by the people, he [Antichrist] shall be proclaimed king. And the Jewish people shall love him much, and he shall reach Jerusalem and raise up their temple."

Antichrist will acknowledge himself to be the Jews' king on their terms, which Jesus would not do. He will accept their flattery and adulation, which Jesus would not do. He will represent himself, which Jesus would not do. As Christ told them so long ago, "I have come in My Father's name, and you do not receive Me; if another comes in his own name, him you will receive" (John 5:43).

The Jews will be the first to declare that, in the person of Antichrist, their "Christ" has finally come. When he receives the ringing endorsement of this traditionally recalcitrant and conservative people, Antichrist's spiritual credentials will attain a sudden and spectacular validity. In order to build on this, he will make Jerusalem his power base. "In this city [Jerusalem] he will establish his kingdom and royal throne in the likeness of David," wrote Saint Andrew of Caesarea.

The present condition of Israel, with its emphasis on nationalism and its rejection of its own truth as revealed in the Torah, indicates to many observers a preparedness, a receptivity to the deception by which they will be taken in. It will be but a short step for Antichrist from being the Christ of the Jews to being the Christ of Christianity as well.

Antichrist will effectively simulate an outer appearance of spirituality. Overwhelmed by this, and by the reports coming from Israel, many Christians will believe that their Lord has returned! It will be the very clamor of such people which sends a signal that the deceiver is at hand. Saint Zosima of Solovetsky Monastery habitually instructed the monks as follows: "When you hear that Christ has come to earth or appeared on earth: then know that this is the antichrist."[15]

As in Noah's Day

One of the most tragic aspects of these developments is that they will be unopposed—they will in fact be unheeded, even by most Christians! Father Boris Molchanoff warns, "The majority of Christians, not being guided by the spiritual mind of the Church, but rather by worldly wisdom, will not perceive this deception and will acknowledge Antichrist as Christ come to earth a second time."[16]

Our Lord Jesus Christ declared that mankind will be generally unprepared for His Return, preoccupied with worldly pursuits. "The days of Noah" are a warning to all: "But as the days of Noah were, so also will the coming of the Son of Man be. For as in the days before the flood, they were eating and drinking, marrying and giving in marriage, until the day that Noah entered the ark, and did not know until the flood came and took them all away, so also will the coming of the Son of Man be" (Matthew 24:37-39).

In this case, the flood that sweeps them away will be a man. Not suspecting Antichrist's real identity and purpose, the masses will openly accept him. Saint John wrote in the Book of Revelation that "all who dwell on the earth will worship him, whose names have not been written in the Book of Life of the Lamb slain from the foundation of the world" (Revelation 13:8).

Saint Gregory the Great expanded on this in his *Moralia*. "When the Antichrist accomplishes the astonishing prodigies before the eyes of all men during his day in the sun, it will not be innumerable men he will capture, it will be all men, all carnal men who seek their delights in the goods, interests, pleasures of this world. Such evil persons will submit themselves to his power without a struggle,—indeed with pleasure."[17]

Capturing "all" men, Antichrist will of course capture all institutions, for these are composed of men. Even religious bodies, or perhaps especially religious bodies, will submit to him as a way of surviving and increasing their power.

To the outward eye, it will seem as though the world has never been so "religious." Spiritual themes will become highly relevant, but they will no longer have Christian meanings. "Spirituality" will serve not to free men, but to enslave them. Fallen churches will be rebuilt in great symbolic grandeur, but within those churches demons will reign.

Elder Lavrenty makes a stunning prediction: "All the churches will be absolutely magnificent, as never before, but one must not go into those churches. Antichrist will be crowned like a king in a grand cathedral in Jerusalem, with the participation of the clergy and the Patriarch. . . . At his coronation, when the Symbol of Faith is read, he will not allow it to be read correctly; where the words describe Jesus Christ as the Son of God, he will renounce this and acknowledge only himself."[18]

Rebuilding the Temple

Antichrist will facilitate the rebuilding of Solomon's temple, both to please the Jews and to erase all doubts that he is their Christ. Saint Andrew of Caesarea insisted that Antichrist will restore the Jewish temple precisely to demonstrate, by fulfilling the Prophet's word, that he is in fact the Messiah: "I will raise up the tabernacle of David, which has fallen down" (Amos 9:11).

Even the present-day official position of the Israeli government is that the Messiah will personally direct the rebuilding of the temple: "According to the [halakah], the Temple will be rebuilt when the Messiah will have come."[19]

But Antichrist's interest in the temple will have a deeper, darker significance. He will secretly envy the prayers ascending to God from the Jews, and will eventually decree that he himself is to be worshiped. Antichrist "comes to the Jews as Christ, and desires to be worshipped by the Jews," insisted Saint Cyril of Jerusalem. "He will make great account of the Temple, that he may more completely beguile them; making it supposed that he is the man of the race of David, who shall build up the Temple which was erected by Solomon."[20]

The Two Witnesses

Two "witnesses" are appointed to appear on earth and expose Antichrist. The Prophet Zechariah calls them olive branches: "What are these two olive branches? . . . These are the two anointed ones, who stand beside the Lord of the whole earth" (Zechariah 4:12, 14).

They will have the power, given by Christ Himself, to prophesy uncontested for three and one-half years, and to defame Antichrist during his first half week: " 'I will give power to my two witnesses,' " declared Christ in the Book of Revelation, " 'and they will prophesy one thousand two hundred and sixty days, clothed in sackcloth.' These are the two olive trees . . . standing before the God of the earth" (Revelation 11:3-5).

These witnesses are considered by Orthodox teachers to be Elias (Elijah) and Enoch, figures whose death has been postponed until the completion of their ministry in the end times. Archbishop Averky explains, "By these two witnesses all the Holy Fathers and teachers of the Church understand almost unanimously the Old Testament righteous ones Enoch and Elias, who were taken alive into heaven."[21]

Malachi predicted long ago that God would send Elias as a warning that the "day of the Lord" was at hand: "Behold, I will send you Elijah the prophet before the coming of the great and dreadful day of the LORD" (Malachi 4:5).

Elias and Enoch were taken up into heaven bodily, and have been preserved until this final confrontation between good and evil, as *The Prologue from Ochrid* explains: "At the end of the world, Elias will appear again, to break the power of antichrist."[22]

The Apostle Jude pointed out that Enoch was the first to proclaim the future coming of the Messiah: "Now Enoch, the seventh from Adam, prophesied about these men also, saying, 'Behold, the Lord comes with ten thousands of His saints, to execute judgment on all'" (Jude 14, 15). And Genesis records that Enoch, like Elias, did not die: "And Enoch walked with God; and he was not, for God took him" (Genesis 5:24).

With mighty works which serve as signs in their own right, they will denounce Antichrist to the world. As Elias stopped the sky from raining in days of old, he will do so again in order to awaken spiritually sleeping man. "These have power to shut heaven, so that no rain falls in the days of their prophecy; and they have power over waters to turn them to blood, and to strike the earth with all plagues, as often as they desire" (Revelation 11:6).

At Elias' prayer, extreme drought will afflict the earth; those who trusted in Antichrist will suffer greatly.

In order to preserve his appearance of goodwill, Antichrist will be forced to endure the reproaches of Enoch and Elias, and put up with the plagues and droughts.

The Apocalypse of Elijah relates that "when Elijah and Enoch hear that the shameless one has appeared in the holy places, they will come down and wage war against him saying, 'Are you not ashamed . . . ? You are the devil.' The shameless one will hear, become angry and wage war against them in the market place of the great city. He will spend seven days fighting with them and kill them. For three and a half days they will lie dead in the market place in full view of all the people. But on the fourth day they will arise again and rebuke him. . . . They will be victorious over the lawless one."[23]

Only at the end of the first "half week," when Antichrist will have attained the fullness of worldly power, will he dare to turn against his accusers. The Synaxarion for Meatfare Sunday reads, "Seven years before [the end of the world], as Daniel foretold, Enoch and Elias will come preaching to them that they not receive him [Antichrist]: Antichrist will torture them and will behead them."

Some have attempted to read other meanings into the miraculous ministry of Enoch and Elias. However, Saint Ephraim the Syrian *(Word on the Coming of the Lord)* and Saint John Damascene *(A Precise Exposition of the Orthodox Faith)* state unequivocally that all which is written concerning these men will actually take place.

Conversion of the Jews

Enoch and Elias will preach in Jerusalem, the Holy City, for three and a half years. As a result of their powerful witness, many Jews will turn to their true Messiah at last. "Behold, I will send you [Jews] Elijah the prophet before the coming of the great and dreadful day of the LORD. And he will turn the hearts of the fathers to the children, and the hearts of the children to their fathers" (Malachi 4:5, 6).

Blessed Theophylactus the Bulgarian wrote, "Elias shall come . . . as the forerunner of the Second Coming, and he shall return to faith in Christ all the Jews who were found to be obedient, remaining faithful, as it were, to the paternal heritage of those who had fallen away therefrom."

This will be one of the most profoundly moving occurrences of the end times. The long vigil of Judaism will end when that "remnant" which the Lord has preserved through the ages finally turns its heart fully to Jesus Christ. "And it shall come to pass in that day that the remnant of Israel . . . will depend on the LORD, the Holy One of Israel, in truth" (Isaiah 10:20).

Thus shall be fulfilled the ancient hope that a remnant, though merely a few grains of all Israel's seas of sand, would truly return to God: "Isaiah also cries out concerning Israel: 'Though the number of the children of Israel be as the sand of the sea, the remnant will be saved' " (Romans 9:27).

The conversion of these Jews will be intense and total: "Then they will look on Me whom they pierced," records Zechariah tenderly. "Yes, they will mourn for Him as one mourns for his only son, and grieve for Him as one grieves for a firstborn" (Zechariah 12:10).

The Book of Revelation assigns a specific number to this remnant: "And I heard the number of those who were sealed. One hundred and forty-four thousand of all the tribes of the children of Israel were sealed" (Revelation 7:4).

The Gospel Preached

Archimandrite Panteleimon wrote that "the Antichrist shall come into the world only when the preaching of the Gospel shall have been spread over the whole universe, when all tribes and peoples shall be enlightened with the light of Christian teaching."[24] This link is affirmed by Saint John of Damascus, who insisted that "it is requisite that the Gospel should be preached among all nations, as the Lord said, and then he will come to refute the impious Jews."[25]

The Great Tribulation will close the door forever upon the "Church age." It is safe to suggest that all human souls will be on one side or the other of the line at that point. The fullness of the Gentiles will have been attained—all those willing to follow Christ to the end will have made their decision. And at that moment, the blindness which has characterized Judaism for thousands of years will be lifted. "For I do not desire, brethren," writes Saint Paul, "that you should be ignorant of this mystery, lest you should be wise in your own opinion, that blindness in part has happened to

Israel until the fullness of the Gentiles has come in" (Romans 11:25).

Over the last three decades many Jews have returned to Christ, and some of these have converted to Orthodoxy, recognizing Orthodox Christianity as the spiritual heir of Judaism. "It is a familiar theme in the conversation and heart of the faithful," wrote Blessed Augustine, "that in the last days before the judgment the Jews shall believe in the true Christ, that is, our Christ, by means of this great and admirable prophet Elias."[26]

The preaching of the gospel will be finalized with the end-times conversion of the Jews. As our Lord indicated when He said, "So the last will be first, and the first last" (Matthew 20:16), this people to whom the Good News was first delivered will also be the last to receive it.

---

[1] *Little Russian Philokalia, Vol. I: St. Seraphim of Sarov,* p. 82.

[2] "Catechetical Lectures," Lecture XV, part 14, in *Nicene and Post-Nicene Fathers,* Vol. VII, p. 108.

[3] *A Ray of Light,* Archimandrite Panteleimon, comp., p. 93.

[4] *Tracts for the Times,* Vol. V, pp. 13, 14, as quoted in Miceli, *The Antichrist,* p. 110.

[5] "Treatise on Christ and Antichrist," in *The Ante-Nicene Fathers,* Vol. V, p. 209.

[6] *The Last Judgement,* pp. 176-177.

[7] "Appendix to the Works of Hippolytus," in *The Ante-Nicene Fathers,* Vol. V, p. 248.

[8] Christensen, *Not of This World,* p. 886.

[9] *The Grand Inquisitor,* p. 12.

[10] "On Miracles and Signs," *Orthodox Life,* Vol. 45, No. 2, March-April 1995, pp. 37-38.

11 "Dies Irae," *Epiphany Journal*, Winter 1983, p. 63.

12 "On Miracles and Signs," *Orthodox Life*, Vol. 45, No. 2, March-April 1995, p. 38.

13 "The Prophetic Gift," *Orthodox America*, October, 1989, p. 6.

14 "On Miracles and Signs," p. 37.

15 St. Ignatius Brianchaninov, "On the Kingdom of God," *Epiphany Journal*, Vol. 9, No. 1, Fall 1988, p. 56.

16 *Antichrist*, p. 5.

17 As paraphrased in Miceli, *The Antichrist*, p. 80.

18 "The Prophetic Gift," *loc. cit.*

19 Quoted in Ice & Price, *Ready to Rebuild*, p. 174.

20 "Catechetical Lectures," Lecture XV, part 15, in *Nicene and Post-Nicene Fathers*, Vol. VII, p. 108.

21 *The Apocalypse of St. John*, p. 128.

22 St. Nicholai Velimirovic, *The Prologue from Ochrid*, Part 3, p. 87.

23 "Dies Irae," *Epiphany Journal*, Winter 1983, p. 64.

24 *A Ray of Light*, p. 42.

25 "An Exact Exposition of the Orthodox Faith," ch. XXVI, in *Nicene and Post-Nicene Fathers*, Vol. IX, p. 98.

26 *The City of God*, Book XX, ch. 29, p. 757.

Chapter 13

The Rapture:
Emancipation or Entrapment?

> *If any person feels within himself a strong heart*
> *to wrestle with Satan, let him remain (for I do*
> *not despair of the Church's strength of nerve), let*
> *him remain and let him say, "Who shall separate*
> *us from the love of Christ?"*
>   —*Saint Cyril of Jerusalem*

On the way to work in the morning, faced with the mundane reality of rush-hour traffic, drivers may find themselves confronted with extraordinary messages. One such is the bumper sticker which admonishes: "WARNING! In the event of Rapture, this car will be left driverless!"

Contemplation of such a scenario produces astounding mental images: Without warning, people begin to float up from the freeway, executives waving briefcases and truckers still clutching C.B. radio microphones, while their abandoned vehicles career wildly or (with God's merciful intervention) coast safely to a stop. The sky is gradually filled with the gently ascending, cheering bodies of the Elect. Below, those who are left behind stare dumbfounded, anxious and resentful. "Who are these people, and why are they flying?" they ask.

Such a visible and large-scale forsaking of the laws of nature cannot be hidden or disguised for long. Sooner or later someone realizes that all the *Christians* are gone! The churches are empty. Only "unbelievers" are left on Planet Earth. After the initial shock, however, these intransigents (why else would they be unbelievers?) go on about their business. "Good riddance!" they snort.

And from this point on, all the grim events of the last days begin to unfold—without any Christians on hand to suffer through them.

Escaping Tribulation

The appeal of "the rapture" to the modern mentality is easy to understand. It is comforting for believers to speculate that they will suddenly and effortlessly be whisked away into heaven without the trouble of dying first. In God's Kingdom they will crowd around the Throne and watch like spectators at a cosmic sporting event as the unfortunate ones remaining on earth endure the Great Tribulation. Having been removed from the playing field before the final period gets underway, they will be impervious to the deceptions and persecutions of Antichrist as he overpowers the whole world.

Because of its promise to spare Christians the

onslaught of the end times, belief in the rapture has attained immense popularity in recent years. Its sudden prominence is less a function of believers' rekindled faith, however, than of its own newness as a doctrine. The rapture was, in fact, unheard of before the nineteenth century, and represents a recent and radical reinterpretation of Scripture. That such a theological reworking has been unquestioningly, even enthusiastically, accepted by a great many people is indicative of a subtle and profound change in contemporary Christian thought, the real effect of which needs to be understood.

Saint Paul's First Epistle to the Thessalonians is generally cited as the primary scriptural basis for the rapture: "We who are alive and remain until the coming of the Lord will by no means precede those who are asleep. For the Lord Himself will descend from heaven with a shout, with the voice of an archangel, and with the trumpet of God. And the dead in Christ will rise first. Then we who are alive and remain shall be caught up ["raptured"] together with them in the clouds to meet the Lord in the air" (1 Thessalonians 4:15-17).

A supporting argument for the rapture is sometimes based on the observation that, in the Revelation of Saint John, the Church is mentioned by name only in the first five chapters, and (supposedly) not at all after the Great Tribulation begins. This is taken to indicate that the Church has been "raptured" into heaven by then.

The most telling critique of this doctrine is simply

the fact of its newness. It developed from a series of visions experienced by a Scottish woman named Margaret Macdonald in 1830. She believed that a "spirit of prophecy" had revealed to her that, prior to Christ's Second Coming, He would come secretly to remove all Christians from the earth. This novel idea was quickly adopted into both Catholic and Protestant doctrines, and spread throughout Europe and America.

Following Macdonald's "visions," Christ's words to the church of Philadelphia were marshaled in support of the "rapture" concept: "I also will keep you from the hour of trial which shall come upon the whole world, to test those who dwell on the earth" (Revelation 3:10). The Lord's High Priestly Prayer shows, however, that He will keep His followers "from the hour of trial" not by removing them from the world, but rather by protecting them from the world's evil: "I do not pray that You should take them out of the world, but that You should keep them from the evil one" (John 17:15).

The concept of Christ rapturing believers was completely unknown during the first thousand years of Christian history, during which time there was but one Christian Faith throughout the world. The Seven Ecumenical Councils of A.D. 325 through 787, in which all the essential doctrines of Christian Truth were declared, never mentioned a rapture.

Father Michael Pomazansky points out the traditional Christian teaching on this subject: that "even the elect will suffer on earth during the 'tribulation' period, and that for their sake this period will be shortened (Matt. 24:21-22)."[1]

It has been suggested by various modern writers that the term "elect" refers not to pre-Tribulation Christians, but to those Jews, allegorically 144,000, who are to convert to Christ in the heat of the last days. But the Scriptures teach otherwise. Saint Peter addresses his first epistle to "the pilgrims of the Dispersion . . . *elect* according to the foreknowledge of God the Father" (1 Peter 1:1, 2, emphasis added). Saint Paul admonishes the Colossian Christians, "Therefore, as the *elect* of God . . . put on tender mercies" (Colossians 3:12, emphasis added). From these passages it is clear that the "elect" are all faithful Christians.

Nor will Christ come secretly, as He Himself declared: "Therefore if they say to you, 'Look . . . He is in the inner rooms!' do not believe it" (Matthew 24:26). The Fathers affirm that the Lord's Return will be unmistakably and suddenly apparent to all mankind: "For as the lightning comes from the east and flashes to the west, so also will the coming of the Son of Man be" (Matthew 24:27).

What Does it Mean?

In order to recapture the traditional understanding of the event Saint Paul is describing to the Thessalonians in the passage quoted earlier, one needs to be clear on when it is to take place. Saint Paul is speaking of the moment of Christ's Second Coming—that is, not before the Great Tribulation, as the rapturists teach, but at the culmination of it: "we who are alive and remain until the coming of the Lord . . ." (1 Thessalonians 4:15).

Saint Matthew is in agreement, and describes the scene in detail: "Immediately after the tribulation of those days the sun will be darkened, and the moon will not give its light; the stars will fall from heaven, and the powers of the heavens will be shaken. Then the sign of the Son of Man will appear in heaven, and then all the tribes of the earth will mourn, and they will see the Son of Man coming on the clouds of heaven with power and great glory. And He will send His angels with a great sound of a trumpet, and they will gather together His elect from the four winds, from one end of heaven to the other" (Matthew 24:29-31).

This being "caught up . . . in the clouds" and being "gather[ed] . . . from the four winds" is a portrayal of the instantaneous spiritual transformation that will occur after the Great Tribulation, when the Lord returns in glory: "We shall not all sleep, but we shall all be changed—in a moment, in the twinkling of an eye, at the last trumpet. For the trumpet will sound, and the dead will be raised incorruptible, and we shall be changed" (1 Corinthians 15:51, 52).

The Countdown
The Word of God cannot fail. Someday everything that is prophesied to happen will happen. "When the transgressors have reached their fullness, a king shall arise, having fierce features, who understands sinister

schemes" (Daniel 8:23). When the time is ripe, Antichrist will arrive on the world stage. He will not appear as a devil, but as a wise benefactor to humanity. Through deception, he will induce virtually all mankind to love and accept him, and even proclaim him king. Everyone will acknowledge his authority because of his apparent goodness and generosity. But once he has attained complete worldly power, he will show his true intent: to compel all people to worship him as god.

Once Antichrist has seized worldwide control of politics, economics, and religion, he will thoroughly and systematically annihilate any resistance to his authority. Then the persecution of those who have not surrendered to him will become so intense that, as the Lord says, "unless those days were shortened, no flesh would be saved" (Matthew 24:22).

Christians will be imprisoned, tortured to make them deny their faith in Christ, brutally murdered, deprived not only of home and sustenance, but even of the means to purchase food. Those will be times of unparalleled horror, of complete spiritual darkness, of such unimaginable suffering that even the communist Gulag was just a dress rehearsal by comparison. It will be the greatest agony of blood and tears that the world has ever seen, or will ever see. "For then there will be great tribulation, such as has not been since the beginning of the world until this time, no, nor ever shall be" (Matthew 24:21).

When these awesome events transpire, what will be the fate of those who have expected the rapture to isolate them from the Great Tribulation? It is safe to assume they will be unprepared to face the crisis. What's worse, they will not understand what is really happening! They will reason that, since they are still on earth, the Antichrist cannot possibly have come yet. This attitude was articulated by the respected Protestant theologian Arthur W. Pink: "The Antichrist cannot appear before the Rapture of the saints," he asserted. As long as the rapture has not yet occurred, "then, here is proof positive that the Antichrist *has not yet appeared*."[2] Not expecting the Deceiver, those awaiting the rapture could be completely taken in by his deception and unwittingly become his disciples.

A Satanic Deception

What could be more diabolically clever than for Antichrist to persuade his victims they need never fear even meeting him? Viewed from this perspective, the common conception of the rapture as a pre-Tribulation "emergency eject" seems to be far more than just a minor misinterpretation of Scripture. It is instead a demonic subterfuge designed to lure many into dangerous complacency. What is more trustworthy—a vision of one person from the nineteenth century or the consensus of the undivided Church of Jesus Christ?

The rapture theory is not so much an outright falsehood as a subtle corruption of truth, a beguiling invitation to be at ease and sleep just when the most stringent wakefulness and caution are needed. Such deception or twisting of God's Word is exactly the technique that Satan, Antichrist's source of power, has used successfully against mankind, beginning in the Garden with Adam and Eve.

Satan's deceptions are beyond mere human ability to resist or even detect. "For false christs and false prophets will rise and show great signs and wonders to deceive, if possible, even the elect" (Matthew 24:24). Whether by astounding miracles or seemingly insignificant distortions of the gospel, Satan continues to dupe humans just as he has from the beginning.

One of Satan's greatest achievements has been to separate people from the living traditions of the Church and to instill in their minds the notion that each person has the right and ability to interpret Scripture for himself. The contemporary concept of the rapture is a logical result of this mistaken attitude.

The Protection of Tradition

Holy Tradition, the living repository of Christ's teachings, has appropriately been called "the life of the Holy Spirit in the Church" (Vladimir Lossky, contemporary Orthodox theologian). Without this Spirit-filled Tradition, the gospel cannot be correctly understood, nor can Satan be defeated.

Saint Basil the Great, writing in the fourth century, declared, "Concerning the teachings of the Church . . . we have received some from written sources, while others have been given to us secretly, through apostolic tradition. Both sources have equal force in true religion.

No one would deny either source—no one, at any rate, who is even slightly familiar with the ordinances of the Church. If we attacked unwritten customs, claiming them to be of little importance, we would fatally mutilate the Gospel."[3]

In these perilous times, it is imperative that Christians look beyond the shallow interpretations and speculations of modernity, to the firm ground of authentic Christian teaching, rooted in the Holy Scriptures. The witness of the Holy Spirit in Christendom is a millennium of unified thought, beginning with the times of the Apostles, upon all the questions which confront believers even today. And it is from this wealth of consistent Christian thought that doctrines such as the rapture can be seen as the dangerous ploys they really are.

[1] *Orthodox Dogmatic Theology*, p. 345.
[2] *The Antichrist*, p. 33.
[3] *On the Holy Spirit*, p. 98.

Chapter 14

The Second Half Week: World Enslavement

The empire of the Romans filled the world, and when the empire fell into the hand of a single person, the world became a dreary place for his enemies. To resist was fatal, and it was impossible to fly.
— *Gibbon, "The Decline and Fall of the Roman Empire"*

"One day the Antichrist will come," wrote Romano Guardini, "a human being who introduces an order of things in which rebellion against God will attain its ultimate power. He will be filled with enlightenment and strength. The ultimate aim of all aims will be to prove that existence without Christ is possible—no, that Christ is the enemy of existence, which can be fully realized only when all Christian values have been destroyed. His arguments will be so impressive, supported by means of such tremendous power—violent and diplomatic, material and intellectual—that to reject them will result in almost insurmountable scandal, and everyone whose eyes are not opened by grace will be lost."[1]

The second half week is the world's last three and a half years; it is that fearful period which Jesus termed the Great Tribulation. When the Antichrist reaches his "fullness" this earth will be as close to hell as it can ever be. Yet, paradoxically, heaven will be right around the corner. The Scriptures have preserved many revealing details about this gruesome time.

Martyrdom of the Two Witnesses

Once Antichrist's hold on power is certain, he will not hesitate to eliminate the great thorns in his side, Elias and Enoch. But even in death these prophets will bear witness to the glory of God.

"When they [Enoch and Elias] finish their testimony, the beast that ascends out of the bottomless pit [Antichrist] will make war against them, overcome them, and kill them," wrote Saint John the Theologian. "And their dead bodies will lie in the street of the great city which spiritually is called Sodom and Egypt, where also our Lord was crucified [Jerusalem]. Then those from the peoples, tribes, tongues, and nations will see their dead bodies three-and-a-half days, and not allow their dead bodies to be put into graves. . . . Now after the three-and-a-half days the breath of life from God entered them, and they stood on their feet, and great fear fell on those who saw them. . . . And they ascended to heaven in a cloud, and their enemies saw them. In the same hour there was a great earthquake, and a tenth of the city fell. In the earthquake seven thousand people were killed, and the rest were afraid and gave glory to the God of heaven" (Revelation 11:7-13).

When Enoch and Elias are gone, no one will be strong enough to raise a protest against the Antichrist. To the worldly, the death of these prophets will be a great relief—the droughts will be ended, the noisy accusations will cease. There will be cause for celebration among the damned.

Mark of the Beast

Many consider the "mark of the beast" to be the most alarming aspect of Antichrist's coming reign. Perhaps this is because the mark is linked to economic activity, and those without it will suffer from the lack of basic necessities. "He causes all, both small and great, rich and poor, free and slave, to receive a mark on their right hand or on their foreheads, and that no one may buy or sell except one who has the mark or the name of the beast, or the number of his name" (Revelation 13:16, 17).

Archimandrite Panteleimon wrote, "A special affliction of people during the reign of Antichrist will be hunger." Saint Nilus cautions Christians to have fortitude: "If you crave and demand food, bear it a little while, and God, having seen your patience, will send you help from above; you will be revived by the aid of the Most High God. If, however, you will not be patient, and will be sealed with the imprint of this foul king, you will later regret this."[2]

It will not be possible to feign either the possession or non-possession of the mark. Its presence or absence will be obvious and irrefutable. Nevertheless, Christians should know that God will provide a way for them to resist. Elder Lavrenty of Russia's Chernigov-Trinity Convent commented, "The mark will be such that it will be immediately apparent whether a person has received it or not. The Christian will not be able to buy or sell anything. But do not despair. The Lord will not abandon His children. One mustn't fear!"[3]

Saint Andrew, Archbishop of Caesarea, wrote, "He will strive so that the mark might be placed upon everyone." Nevertheless, those who want to remain faithful to Christ must refuse the mark, for it absolutely and permanently links a soul to Satan.

Saint John tells us, "Then a third angel followed them, saying with a loud voice, 'If anyone worships the beast and his image, and receives his mark on his forehead or on his hand, he himself shall also drink of the wine of the wrath of God' " (Revelation 14:9).

Under economic duress, Christians will be strongly tempted to think that they can receive the mark of the beast without being harmed thereby. They will reason, "Of what benefit is it to refuse if we starve? The mark on our flesh will not affect the faith in our hearts."

The Russian New Martyr Bishop Damascene specifically addressed this argument, pointing out that for Christians it is not possible to accept the mark anywhere. "Why is it that the seal of Antichrist . . . will be placed not upon the forehead and the hand

simultaneously, but upon the forehead *or* the hand? . . .
This will occur because at that time there will be people
who will affirm that it is possible and permissible to
recognize the God-fighting authority of Antichrist if
only one remains a Christian in one's soul. From such
ones Antichrist will not demand that they share his way
of thinking; in other words, upon all such ones he will
not place the seal on their forehead, but will demand of
them only the recognition of his authority, which is,
according to St. Hippolytus, the seal on the hand. . . .
A Christian by this very fact will cut off from himself
every possibility of doing good and righteous deeds, for
in his faith there will be missing the chief sign of
uprightness—the confession of God as God and the
recognition of Him as the Being that stands above
all. . . . Repentance is impossible for such ones, according to the teaching of the Holy Church; and it is
impossible only because the seal of Christ and the seal
of Antichrist are incompatible with each other, and the
reception of one banishes the presence of the other."[4]

But what is the purpose of the mark? Saint Ephraim
the Syrian considered that it is to prevent people from
making the sign of the Cross, which is especially fearful
to Antichrist. This is why the mark is placed on the
forehead or right hand, both used in making the holy
sign. "Let everyone show the sign of the honorable
Cross, making its sign at all times," exhorted Saint
Nilus, "for the sign of the Cross frees man from the
suffering of hell; but the seal of Antichrist leads man to
the suffering of hell."[5]

The Plagues

Part of the utopian ideal is the elimination of disease and bodily misery. As medical technologies are developed more and more, it will seem that man has learned to accomplish miracles. Yet in the end times, he will be humbled by deadly epidemics beyond his control.

"Truly no one in that time will suspect that the world is coming to an end or will imagine in what hour the Son of Man will come and so mankind will be taken unaware," we read in *Apostasy and Antichrist*. "Progress will have reached an apex and the fight against illnesses and disease will be reaching such an advanced stage that it will seem as if even death would soon be conquered. Then, suddenly the vessels of wrath will be poured out upon the followers of Antichrist: sores and boils will afflict those bearing the mark of the beast and the waters of the earth will be turned to blood."[6]

The Book of Revelation speaks of "death" riding a pale horse, and of a "vial of wrath" poured out upon the earth. These messengers of misery will send plagues of disease and sickness to those in league with Antichrist. "I looked, and behold, a pale horse. And the name of him who sat on it was Death, and Hades followed with him. And power was given to them over a fourth of the earth, to kill with sword, with hunger, with death, and by the beasts of the earth" (Revelation 6:8).

Yet, rather than acknowledging that their sin against God has drawn down these tortures, men will condemn even more their own Creator. Saint Nilus the

Myrrhstreaming said, "The more calamities afflict them, the more evil will they become; instead of repenting, they will be angered at God. The evil deeds of people will surpass those of people at the time of the flood. All will speak only of evil, plan only evil, consent to evil, meet others only for evil."[7]

The wrath of God will afflict the world, yet few will repent. "Then I heard a loud voice from the temple saying to the seven angels, 'Go and pour out the bowls of the wrath of God on the earth.' So the first went and poured out his bowl upon the earth, and a foul and loathsome sore came upon the men who had the mark of the beast and those who worshiped his image. Then the second angel poured out his bowl on the sea, and it became blood as of a dead man; and every living creature in the sea died. Then the third angel poured out his bowl on the rivers and springs of water, and they became blood. . . . Then the fourth angel poured out his bowl on the sun. . . . And men were scorched with great heat, and they blasphemed the name of God who has power over these plagues; and they did not repent and give Him glory. Then the fifth angel poured out his bowl on the throne of the beast, and his kingdom became full of darkness; and they gnawed their tongues because of the pain. They blasphemed the God of heaven because of their pains and their sores, and did not repent of their deeds" (Revelation 16:1-11).

Paradoxically, this suffering is a sign of God's mercy. It is a witness that the world is neither perfect nor perfectible. Man cannot find complete happiness in it, for even if all diseases were conquered, death would nonetheless eventually claim its prize. Man wishes to push away every suggestion that he is mortal, while doing little to gain true immortality. But God gives him wounds and pain and grief as an inescapable reminder that real peace can never be found here, but only in heaven.

Desolation of the Temple

When the world has acknowledged him as divine, the impostor, also known as the "abomination of desolation," will enter the rebuilt Jewish temple, and install himself in the Holy of Holies as the object of worship!

Then will the words of our Lord Jesus Christ be fulfilled: " 'Therefore when you see the "abomination of desolation," spoken of by Daniel the prophet, standing in the holy place' (whoever reads, let him understand), 'then let those who are in Judea flee to the mountains. Let him who is on the housetop not go down to take anything out of his house. And let him who is in the field not go back to get his clothes. But woe to those who are pregnant and to those who are nursing babies in those days! And pray that your flight may not be in winter or on the Sabbath. For then there will be great tribulation' " (Matthew 24:15-21).

The Prophet Daniel foresaw that Antichrist will elevate himself even against God, and shall enjoy total worldly success in this regard. "Then the king shall do according to his own will: he shall exalt and magnify himself above every god, shall speak blasphemies against the God of gods, and shall prosper till the wrath has been accomplished" (Daniel 11:36).

Persecution of Believers

Having seized all earthly power, political, economic, and spiritual, Antichrist will have finally become absolutely invincible. For what secular power would dare to cross "God's anointed"? From this point on he will show no mercy on his enemies. All believers in the true God will suffer then, either by direct persecution, or by the rigors of flight and hiding. "After these two [Enoch and Elias] have been slain, he will then persecute the rest of the faithful, either by making them glorious martyrs or by rendering them apostates," wrote Monk Adso in the eleventh century.[8]

Any churches still worshiping Christ will be targeted for destruction. The barbaric techniques which were developed in communist regimes will reach their sadistic perfection under Antichrist. Religious buildings will be closed, priests murdered, believers imprisoned or exiled. It will become impossible to pray openly. Religious literature will be confiscated and church services forbidden.

As Antichrist placed himself in the Holy of Holies of the Jewish temple, he will do something similar in Christian churches, in order to encourage a cult of adoration. He will make himself the object of worship instead of Christ. Icons, crucifixes, and other symbols of Jesus Christ will be removed and replaced by demonic images, which all people will be ordered to worship.

Antichrist will bring to fruition the war against God which has smoldered as the "mystery of lawlessness" for centuries. He will carry the battle to those remaining faithful to their Lord, and many will die. "It was granted to him to make war with the saints and to overcome them. And authority was given him over every tribe, tongue, and nation" (Revelation 13:7).

But God loves His children, and has forewarned them what to expect. The difficulties will be great, but it *will* be possible to resist Antichrist.

The Seventh Church

Along with a unified world government, a single world religion will emerge, supposedly based on the best principles of many religions, but particularly mocking Christianity. A desire for peace and unity on a superficial level will make many people vulnerable to this religion, especially since Antichrist will be its head.

Dostoevsky created a brilliant foreimage of the Antichrist type in his Grand Inquisitor. Reflecting on man's nature, the Grand Inquisitor contemptuously offers these comments: "So long as man remains free he strives for nothing so incessantly and so painfully as to find some one to worship. But man seeks to worship what is established beyond dispute, so that all men would agree at once to worship it. For these pitiful creatures are concerned not only to find what one or the other can worship, but to find something that all would believe in and worship; what is essential is that all may be *together* in it."[9]

Just when Christians are most in need of the true Church, they will find that, with few exceptions, the "churches" are in the hands of the enemy. The visible organization of religions, being a worldly structure, will have been infiltrated by Antichrist.

"One must suppose that the structure of the Church, which has long been wavering, will collapse terribly and quickly," wrote Saint Ignatius Brianchaninov. "There is no one to stop or oppose this. The means adopted to support it are borrowed from the elements of the world which are hostile to the Church and will hasten its fall rather than prevent it."[10]

The few true Christians who remain must avoid those places as spiritual deathtraps. Elder Lavrenty predicted, "There will be churches, but Orthodox Christians must not go into them, because the Bloodless Sacrifice of Jesus Christ will not be offered there; instead, there will be satanic gatherings."[11]

The seventh and last church period, as described in the third chapter of Revelation, belongs to the period of Antichrist's reign. For this church, Laodicea, our Lord has only condemnation: "I know your works, that you are neither cold nor hot. I could wish you were cold or hot. So then, because you are lukewarm, and neither cold nor hot, I will vomit you out of My mouth. Because you say, 'I am rich, have become wealthy, and have need of nothing'—and do not know that you are wretched, miserable, poor, blind, and naked—I counsel you to buy from Me gold refined in the fire, that you may be rich; and white garments, that you may be clothed, that the shame of your nakedness may not be revealed; and anoint your eyes with eye salve, that you may see" (Revelation 3:15-18).

"To . . . the church of Laodicea . . . the Lord does not utter . . . a single favorable word," wrote Archbishop Averky. ". . . The church of Laodicea [represents] the last, most frightful epoch before the end of the world, characterized by indifference to the faith and outward prosperity."[12]

But in His mercy, Christ our God makes a promise. To those of Laodicea who repent and turn to Him he says, "Behold, I stand at the door and knock. If anyone hears My voice and opens the door, I will come in to him and dine with him, and he with Me" (Revelation 3:20).

Persevering to the End

So evil will those times be that few will escape Antichrist's snare. Even those who actually recognize him will be hard pressed to withstand. Father Seraphim Rose wrote, "Many who recognize the Antichrist when he comes will nonetheless worship him—only the power of Christ given to the heart will have strength to resist him."[13]

The majority of peoples and earthly nations at that time will be united in their rejection of God, and will hate anyone who believes in Christ. "Then they will deliver you up to tribulation and kill you, and you will be hated by all nations for My name's sake. And then many will be offended, will betray one another, and will hate one another" (Matthew 24:9, 10).

Yet in spite of intense persecution, true Christians will not submit to Satan. They will be considered treasonous, will be hounded and hunted, accused of being criminals, psychopaths, even enemies of God Himself! "Yes, the time is coming," promised Jesus, "that whoever kills you will think that he offers God service" (John 16:2).

Christians will suffer so intensely that it may seem God has abandoned His children. But when the darkness is deepest, the Lord will return! Saint John Maximovitch wrote, "And in the days of great sorrow . . . the remnant of the faithful are to experience in themselves something like that which was experienced once by the Lord Himself when He, hanging on the Cross, being perfect God and perfect Man, felt Himself so forsaken by His Divinity that He cried out to Him: 'My God, my God, Why hast Thou forsaken me?' The last Christians also will experience in themselves a similar abandonment of humanity by the grace of God, but only for a very short time, after the passing of which the Lord will not delay immediately to appear in all His glory, and all the holy Angels with Him. And then will be performed in all its fullness everything foreordained from the ages in the pre-eternal counsel (of the Holy Trinity)."[14]

Who will stand up as a Christian in the face of this horror? Saint Ephraim the Syrian puts the question more bluntly: "Who, brethren, will then prove to be guarded, unshakable . . . when he beholds the unspeakable afflictions which will come from every direction upon every soul . . . who will persevere when he beholds the whole world in turmoil, everyone fleeing to hide himself in the mountains and some dying from hunger, others melting like wax from thirst. . . .

"Who will endure the insufferable affliction when he sees the gathering of the peoples who will come from the ends of the earth to see the tormentor? . . . Who will have such an adamantine soul as to endure all these temptations? Where, as I said, will such a man be found whom all the angels would bless?"

It will be a time of great testing, when to go against Antichrist will be to go against the peer pressure of the whole world. And yet, there will be those who do just that. "Many shall be purified, made white, and refined, but the wicked shall do wickedly; and none of the wicked shall understand, but the wise shall understand" (Daniel 12:10).

Although the Lord promises to be with those who trust in Him, he does not say they will have no difficulties. Just the opposite, for in bidding us to take up our crosses and follow Him, He offers us a share not only in His heavenly glory, but in His earthly sufferings as well.

The Path to Resurrection

"Let not us, who would be Christians, expect anything else from it than to be crucified," wrote Father Seraphim Rose. "For to be Christian is to be crucified, in this time and in any time since Christ came for the first time. His life is the example—and warning—to us all. We must be crucified personally, mystically; for through crucifixion is the only path to resurrection. If we would rise with Christ, we must first be humbled with Him— even to the ultimate humiliation, being devoured and spit forth by the uncomprehending world.

"And we must be crucified outwardly, in the eyes of the world; for Christ's Kingdom is not of this world, and the world cannot bear it, even a single representative of it, even for a single moment. The world can only accept Antichrist, now or at any time."[15]

The end-times martyrs will be the most fortunate of all humans, for they will defy Antichrist to his face. Blessed surely he who shall then be a martyr for Christ! "I say that the Martyrs of that time excel all martyrs," wrote Saint Cyril of Jerusalem. "For the martyrs hitherto have wrestled with men only; but in the time of Antichrist they shall do battle with Satan in his own person."[16]

To the weakest of all Christians shall be given history's most awesome challenge: to proclaim the Truth in a culture totally given over to apostasy. In this world they will be treated like dirt, but in heaven they will shine like the brightest stars. "O blessed ones, count whatever is hard in this lot of yours as a discipline of your powers of mind and body," encouraged Tertullian. "You are about to pass through a noble struggle . . . in which the prize is an eternal crown of angelic essence, citizenship in the heavens, glory everlasting."[17]

[1] *The Lord*, p. 513.
[2] *A Ray of Light*, pp. 59, 83.
[3] "The Prophetic Gift," *Orthodox America*, October 1989, p. 6.
[4] "The Seal of Christ and the Seal of Antichrist," quoted in I.M. Andreyev, *Russia's Catacomb Saints*, pp. 222-223.
[5] *A Ray of Light*, p. 83.
[6] *Apostasy and Antichrist*, p. 41.
[7] Quoted in *A Ray of Light*, p. 67.
[8] *Apocalyptic Spirituality*, Bernard McGinn, trans., p. 96.
[9] *The Grand Inquisitor*, p. 9.
[10] Quoted in Archbishop Averky, *Stand Fast in the Truth*, p. 5.
[11] "The Prophetic Gift," *loc. cit.*
[12] *The Apocalypse of St. John*, pp. 72, 76.
[13] Christensen, *Not of This World*, p. 652.
[14] *The Orthodox Word*, 1973, No. 50, pp. 123-124.
[15] *Not of This World*, p. 149.
[16] "Catechetical Lectures," Lecture XV, part 17, in *The Ante-Nicene Fathers*, Vol. VII, p. 109.
[17] "Ad Martyras," in *The Ante-Nicene Fathers*, Vol. III, p. 694.

Chapter 15

The Catacomb Church

*For the True Orthodox Church there was left no
alternative but to go into the catacombs. . . .*
—I.M. Andreyev

The Epistles and Acts of the Apostles are eloquent
witnesses that being a Christian in the first days of the
Church was no picnic. "I die daily," declared Saint Paul
(1 Corinthians 15:31), and he went on to enumerate
beatings, flailings, stonings, imprisonments, and other
assaults on his life.

Pagan Rome was a type or premonition of that
future godless kingdom which Antichrist shall establish. The last Roman Empire, like the first, is destined
to be overwhelmingly hostile to the few Christians in
its midst. "Christianity began as the religion of a small
minority existing in a predominantly non-Christian
society, and such it is becoming once more," warns
Bishop Kallistos Ware of England.[1]

Christians of the end times must learn what their
brethren of the Church's earliest years knew well—how
to suffer. As Saint Paul reminded young Timothy, "All
who desire to live godly in Christ Jesus will suffer

persecution" (2 Timothy 3:12). God's gift of salvation in heaven does not necessarily improve one's earthly situation; it merely renders it irrelevant. "It is of no consequence where you are in the world—you who are not of it," Tertullian pointed out.[2]

A Heritage of Martyrdom

For the first few centuries of the Church's life, Rome was the source of the most intense persecutions. Saints Peter and Paul were both martyred in the imperial capital on June 29, A.D. 67 or 68. Peter was crucified upside down, and Paul was beheaded.

As the decades and centuries passed, countless believers also gave their lives for their convictions while a succession of emperors vainly struggled to eradicate the Church. Nero illuminated his gardens at night with living Christian torches. In about A.D. 200 Septimius Severus, who had already made conversion to Judaism an offense in Palestine, prohibited propagation of, and conversion to, Christianity.

In A.D. 250 Decius ordered all Roman subjects to renounce Christ and to participate in pagan religious ceremonies. Diocletian, who considered himself a god, initiated the most savage persecution in A.D. 303. Imprisonment, torture and execution became routine. While the stone walls of the Coliseum resounded with inhuman, demonic cheers, Christian blood flowed.

But none of this succeeded. Since they had something real to die for, Christians were emboldened rather than intimidated by torture. "Christ's opponents always achieve results opposite to those that their actions against Christ would [lead one to] expect," wrote recently canonized Saint Nicholai Velimirovic. "Instead of blocking the river of Christianity, they widen it and deepen it, and make the roar of its flow heard the more clearly. Instead of drying it up, they produce a veritable flood of Christianity across the whole world."[3]

Frightening though those times of terror were, they could not destroy the Church. On the contrary, they actually strengthened it by providing Christians with dramatic and conclusive opportunities to give their all for God. "The oftener we are mown down by you, the more in number we grow," Tertullian cried to the pagans. "The blood of Christians is seed!"[4] And as that "seed" sprang up, it raised additional heroes of the Faith, men and women eager to lose the lesser in order to gain the greater, to sacrifice the temporal for the eternal.

"Beloved, do not think it strange concerning the fiery trial which is to try you, as though some strange thing happened to you," counseled Saint Peter; "but rejoice to the extent that you partake of Christ's sufferings, that when His glory is revealed, you may also be glad with exceeding joy. If you are reproached for the name of Christ, blessed are you, for the Spirit of glory and of God rests upon you" (1 Peter 4:12-14).

Indeed, the martyrs often evinced a fear not that they would suffer, but that they would be prevented from doing so. Saint Ignatius the "God-bearer" is a perfect example of this. Ignatius learned to love Christ at an early age, for Tradition teaches he was the child our Lord held when He said, "Therefore whoever humbles himself as this little child is the greatest in the kingdom of heaven" (Matthew 18:4).

After a life of service to God, Saint Ignatius was sent to Rome to be condemned. Along the way, he implored his fellow Christians not to impede his martyrdom by any prayer or action. "I desire nothing," he said, "either visible or invisible, but to come to Christ."[5]

Where did Saint Ignatius get such strength of spirit? As soldiers were leading him to the arena to be eaten by lions, they asked why he constantly voiced the name of Jesus. He replied that God's name had been written in his heart through his lifelong habit of repeating the Jesus Prayer: "Lord Jesus Christ, Son of God, have mercy on me, a sinner."

Also called the prayer of the Publican ("God, be merciful to me a sinner" from Luke 18:13), the Jesus Prayer was central to the inner discipline of ancient Christians. "Eventually," relates Paul Allen, "after long practice, this sinks into the heart as 'praying without ceasing,' whether asleep or awake."[6] Thus it fulfilled Saint Paul's command to "pray without ceasing" (1 Thessalonians 5:17).

Unseen Warfare records that the prayer was recommended by "St. Ephrem, St. Chrysostom, St. Isaac of Syria, St. Hesychius, St. Barsanuphius and John, and St. John of the Ladder. Later it became more and more general, began to be on everyone's lips and became part of the Church's statutes, where it is offered in place of all prayers said at home and of all church services."[7]

Repetition of the words "Lord Jesus Christ, Son of God, have mercy on me, a sinner" can produce such a profoundly prayerful disposition that in time the words continue to be voiced in the heart without further effort. Bishop Kallistos Ware explained this phenomenon: "When a man begins to pray, at first he prays with the lips, and has to make a conscious intellectual effort in order to realize the meaning of what he says. But if he perseveres, praying continually with recollection, his intellect and his heart become united. . . . The prayer fills the entire consciousness, and no longer has to be forced out, but says itself. This Prayer of the Heart cannot be attained simply through our own efforts, but is a gift conferred by the grace of God."[8]

Christianity a Paradox

The lives of holy martyrs demonstrate that Christianity contains a mystery, an apparent contradiction. How can hope flourish in the midst of horror? How is it possible to choose death rather than to deny or betray Christ? How may we worship this God who has become Man—a Man who was executed as a criminal at that? How can the Cross, a sign of ignominy, become instead the symbol of victory and honor?

Leonid Ouspensky described the paradox in these terms: "The Cross is then the concrete expression of the Christian mystery, of victory by defeat, of glory by humiliation, of life by death—symbol of an omnipotent God, Who willed to become man and to die as a slave, in order to save His creature."[9]

The paradoxes of Christianity range from the historical to the doctrinal. The Lord taught that "the last will be first, and the first last" (Matthew 20:16), and Saint Paul declared that "the wisdom of this world is foolishness with God" (1 Corinthians 3:19). Even opponents recognized this, for the idol-worshipers of Thessalonica complained, "These who have turned the world upside down have come here too" (Acts 17:6).

Saint Gregory of Nazianzus wrote in the fourth century, "As a sheep He is led to the slaughter, but He is the Shepherd of Israel, and now of the whole world also. As a Lamb He is silent, yet He is the Word, and is proclaimed by the Voice of one crying in the wilderness. He is bruised and wounded, but He healeth every disease and every infirmity. He is lifted up and nailed to the Tree, but by the Tree of Life He restoreth us."[10]

The Church makes no attempt to resolve this spiritual mystery in a material fashion, or according to human logic. Instead, she opens the eyes of her children to faith and wisdom, and bestows a vision which, encompassing more than this earthly domain, reaches into heaven itself.

Not of This World

From the Holy Spirit Christians receive that otherworldly perspective in which living may equal dying and death may equal life. For a Christian, "right faith" (Orthodoxy) is not an intellectual conceit, but something worth dying for. This is because the Truth underlying Christian doctrine is not some abstract formula, but a Person—a God who is able to save souls.

Christians are called to die to themselves, whether that results in physical death or not. "When you desire to do something for love of God, put death as the limit of your desire," taught Saint Isaac of Syria in the seventh century. "In this way you will rise in actual deed to the level of martyrdom in struggling with every passion, suffering no harm from whatever you may meet within this limit, if you endure to the end and do not weaken."

Giving all for the Faith has always meant enduring some degree of isolation, ridicule, and estrangement from the society of man. This is not an easy task, and there is always the danger of complacency and compromise with worldliness. In apostolic times, as now, Christ called His followers to be on guard against this. To maintain such vigilance requires a strong Christian community.

Christianity is only possible in the context of the Church, in the company of other believers. In the Church's formative years Christians came together to share the *agape* meal, to celebrate the Eucharist, to commune with one another and with the saints. Since official persecution prevented meeting in public places for worship, believers met in private homes, or sometimes in the catacombs.

To pagans the catacombs were nothing more than underground graveyards, which they regarded with superstitious horror. To Christians, however, the catacombs were places where the communal life of the

Church could be practiced unhindered by the authorities. While the mazes and tombs cut into the soft rock at the city's outskirts afforded believers some concealment, more importantly, they enabled Christians to stand together with departed saints on holy ground.

The Allure of the Catacombs

The catacombs cannot be explained away as simply being discreet places to meet. They suggest a mystery: Why did the children of Light commune in earthly darkness? Why did those newly born into Christ's Life mingle among the tombs of unhallowed dead? Again, Christianity's enigma perplexes the worldly mind, and only the heart of faith may fully understand.

As martyrs fell, these public cemeteries became the repositories of holy relics. The bodies of Saints Peter and Paul, along with many others, were interred in such subterranean labyrinths along Rome's Appian Way. The Liturgy was celebrated directly over their graves, and the Communion of Christ's Body and Blood became a daily act of preparation by believers for the Lord's Return. Saint Paul had reminded them that by doing this "you proclaim the Lord's death till He comes" (1 Corinthians 11:26).

Liturgy is the communal labor of devotion and prayer to God. *Leitourgia*, which literally means "the work of the people," is, in the words of contemporary writer Benjamin Williams, "that celebration of the church, which has its origins in God's revelation, by which believers worship God and in the process are formed into the church. That is why the Eucharist is the focal point of the liturgy; it is in the Eucharist that we receive New Life by the grace of God."[11]

During the Liturgy, invocations were commonly offered to the newly arrived citizens of heaven. Some of these prayers, scratched into the stone, can be seen even today. Prayer to the saints was a natural extension of normal brotherly communication. Since it was common to ask for the prayers and blessings of living Christians, how much better to ask the same of them once they had gone to the Lord?

The Cloud of Witnesses

Those who had gone to their rest in the Lord were elder brothers and sisters in the Faith. Although a formidable and dangerous gulf existed between heaven and earth, the saints had bridged it by climbing Jacob's Ladder, a symbol for Christ Himself. And through the Lord, the Church Triumphant (the saints in heaven) and the Church Militant (those remaining on earth) were united in a bond that permitted and encouraged conversation between all parties. The "cloud of witnesses" of which Saint Paul spoke (Hebrews 12:1) was ever present among those who belonged to God. While for pagans the afterlife was a vast and frightening unknown, for Christians it was going home to friends and family.

Not only could Christians on earth pray with their departed friends in the Faith, they might well expect to receive assistance in return. "The Church in this world and the next is one Church, one body, one being; as the root of a tree beneath the earth is one organism with its trunk and branches above the earth," wrote Saint Nicholai Velimirovic. "From this it is clear how we, being part of the Church on earth, can receive help from the saints in the Church in heaven."[12]

The Catacomb Church ultimately came to represent not just a place, but a foretaste of heaven itself. It provided communion with the Lord and His servants, which prepared believers to face and overcome evil. It taught Christians that heaven is only gained through suffering on earth, as Lutheran pastor Richard Wurmbrand emphasizes: "You can be baptized and you can believe, but you will not be a member of the Underground Church unless you know how to suffer."[13]

Although Christians eventually worshiped in grand buildings, the spirit of the early catacombs never died. With Constantine's conversion to Christianity, writes Bishop Kallistos Ware, "the age of the martyrs and the persecutions drew to an end, and the Church of the Catacombs became the Church of the Empire."[14]

This marked a period of expansion in which millions were drawn to Christ. With the growth of worshipers, new houses of worship needed to be built. For example, above Rome's clandestine catacombs rose a basilica dedicated to Saints Peter and Paul, whose relics lay beneath it. Renamed the Church of San Sebastian years later, this structure still stands near the beginning of the Appian Way.

An Image Yet to Come

Saint Andrew of Caesarea considered that the catacomb spirit of the early Church would be particularly
necessary during the end times: "And so it is always, but
especially at the coming of antichrist who will reign for
three and one-half years. At that time it may be there
will escape from him those who have hidden in the
literal wilderness—the mountains, holes and caves."

For the last Christians, hiding for their faith will
kindle archetypal memories of those first believers in
ancient Rome. The Church which overcomes will become again what it was then—a place to live and die for
Christ. As Archbishop Averky stated, Orthodox Christians must "prepare for catacomb times ahead. . . .
Soviet Russia already gives us an example of what we
may expect—only worse, for the times do not get
better."[15]

Christians in Soviet Russia have surely had the most
recent experience of catacomb life. In order to escape
the false "unity" of communism, they had to "separate"
and meet outside official channels. Here they found
real Christian communion—not the outer unity of
false ecumenism, but the inner unity of the Holy Spirit.
This Christian communion has nothing to do with
institutions; it transcends cultural, economic and political boundaries, and will become more and more
evident as the last days unfold.

Before Soviet communism collapsed, a witness of
the remnant Church in Russia reported: "The Easter
service was held in an apartment of an official State

institution. Entrance was possible only with a special pass, which I obtained for myself and for my small daughter. About thirty people were present, among them some of my acquaintances. An old priest celebrated the service, which I shall never forget. 'Christ is risen' we sang softly, but full of joy. . . . The joy that I felt in this service . . . gives me strength to live, even today."[16]

Finding the Catacomb Church

Satan strives to capture humanity not because he loves man, but because he hates God. Many ignorantly follow the one who will destroy them, as Jesus warned: "For wide is the gate and broad is the way that leads to destruction, and there are many who go in by it" (Matthew 7:13).

On the other hand, a small number will overcome and reject Satan's thrall. "Narrow is the gate and difficult is the way which leads to life, and there are few who find it" (Matthew 7:14). It is these few upon whom Antichrist will focus his greatest rage, for their very existence bears witness to Christ's victory over him.

So long as one believer remains, the true Church has not vanished from the earth and Antichrist's claim to rule over all is false. The evil one is willing to consume even the child issuing from its mother's womb, if by so doing he can prevent another Christian soul from worshiping the true God.

The Lord promises that His Church will always exist: "I will build My church, and the gates of Hades shall not prevail against it" (Matthew 16:18). Yet, when every institution has been penetrated and corrupted by the evil one, where will Christ's Bride reside? The Book of Revelation offers a clear vision of this:

"Now a great sign appeared in heaven: a woman clothed with the sun, with the moon under her feet, and on her head a garland of twelve stars. Then being with child, she cried out in labor and in pain to give birth. And another sign appeared in heaven: behold, a great, fiery red dragon having seven heads and ten horns, and seven diadems on his heads. His tail drew a third of the stars of heaven and threw them to the earth. And the dragon stood before the woman who was ready to give birth, to devour her Child as soon as it was born. She bore a male Child who was to rule all nations with a rod of iron. And her Child was caught up to God and His throne" (Revelation 12:1-5).

Saint Hippolytus, Saint Methodius, and Saint Andrew of Caesarea affirm that this woman represents the Church of Christ. Archbishop Averky explains, "[The] torments of birthgiving signify the difficulties which had to be overcome by the Church of Christ when it was being established in the world (martyrdom, the spreading of heresies). . . . By [the] stars which the devil draws after himself in his fall, commentators understand the fallen angels or demons. . . . The Church always gives birth to Christ through men, and from the very beginning Satan has striven to devour Christ as he did in the person of Herod. . . . The Lord Jesus Christ was caught up to heaven on the day of His glorious ascension and sat upon the throne of His Father. . . . So also are all Christians of the last times to be caught up *to meet the Lord in the air* (I Thess. 4:17)."[17]

Flight to the Wilderness

Saint John the Apostle teaches in the Book of Revelation that during the times of Antichrist this woman, the Holy Church, will flee "into the wilderness," where God will provide for her: "Then the woman fled into the wilderness, where she has a place prepared by God, that they should feed her there one thousand two hundred and sixty days. . . . Now when the dragon saw that he had been cast to the earth, he persecuted the woman who gave birth to the male Child. But the woman was given two wings of a great eagle, that she might fly into the wilderness to her place, where she is nourished for a time and times and half a time, from the presence of the serpent" (Revelation 12:6, 13, 14).

That she will be persecuted by the dragon for "one thousand two hundred and sixty days" and for "a time and times and half a time" shows clearly that the Church and her members will be present and suffer during the three and a half years of the Great Tribulation. Nevertheless, God will give her the means to hide and to survive, and this accounts for her perceived absence. Saint John Maximovitch explains, "The *Apocalypse* represents the fate of the Church in the image of a woman who hides herself in those times in the wilderness: she does not show herself in public life."[18]

Fleeing cities and "civilization," those remaining faithful to Christ will seek the isolation and consolation of nature. "Then let those who are in Judea flee to the mountains," urged Jesus (Matthew 24:16). Once there, they shall "begin 'to say to the mountains, "Fall on us!" and to the hills, "Cover us!" ' " (Luke 23:30).

Isaiah also predicted an exodus of believers. "They shall go into the holes of the rocks, and into the caves of the earth, from the terror of the LORD and the glory of His majesty, when He arises to shake the earth mightily" (Isaiah 2:19).

The Prophet advises them to take shelter from the "indignation" during Satan's "little moment" of release, for at that time God's wrath will punish all those who have followed the beast: "Come, my people, enter your chambers, and shut your doors behind you; hide yourself, as it were, for a little moment, until the indignation is past. For behold, the LORD comes out of His place to punish the inhabitants of the earth for their iniquity" (Isaiah 26:20, 21).

Even as the first true Christians, afflicted and martyred by pagans, hid in graveyard catacombs for sanctuary, so is it prophesied that the last Christians will take refuge in rocks and forests, the "catacombs" of the wilderness, in order to preserve themselves from the neo-pagans of the apostate man of sin. "For then there will be found many people who had pleased God and who may be able to be saved in the hills and desert places by many prayers and ceaseless lamentation," wrote Saint Ephraim. "For Holy God, seeing their indescribable weeping and true faith, will show them mercy, like a tender father, and will watch over them wherever they will hide."[19]

The Mind of the Fathers

The life of the catacomb Church must be formed by oneness of soul within the mind of the Fathers. According to Father Seraphim Rose, *"To practice love, trust, and life according to the Holy Fathers in the small circle where one is*—there seems to be no other way to solve the 'spiritual crisis' of today which expresses itself in absence of oneness of soul and mind. If one finds the *mind of the Fathers,* then one will be at one with the others who find it also."[20]

And a group even of two or three, as the Lord said, within the mind of the Fathers, constitutes the Church. "A pillar of the Church is every true believer who adheres to the Tradition of the Fathers in spite of all the frightful currents of the world which attempt to pull him away," says Alexander Kalomiros. "Such pillars will exist until the end of the world, whatever might happen."[21]

Saint John Chrysostom declared that even if only one of these pillars remains standing, the Church will not fall, for "nothing is stronger than the Church." In concert with this theme, Saint John Maximovitch said, "In times of trouble, each Christian is himself responsible for the fullness of Christianity . . . each member of the Orthodox Church is responsible for the whole Church."[22]

But how specifically can this be? The process begins in one's own heart, with the desire to serve Christ at any cost and to die for Him if necessary. Then one seeks out those of like mind in the Faith.

Lutheran pastor Richard Wurmbrand, who spent fourteen years in a communist slave labor camp because of his faith in Christ, believes preparation for hardship must be communicated to Christians early in life. "I took a group of ten to fifteen boys and girls on a Sunday morning, not to a church, but to the zoo," he once related. "Before the cage of lions I told them, 'Your forefathers in faith were thrown before such wild beasts for their faith. Know that you also will have to suffer. You will not be thrown before lions, but you will have to do with men who would be much worse than lions. Decide here and now if you wish to pledge allegiance to Christ.' They had tears in their eyes when they said, 'Yes.' We have to make the preparation now, before we are imprisoned."[23]

Preparing for Eternity

The goal of Christians should not be physical survival *per se,* but the survival of faith in Christ. The Lord will preserve His Church even against hell. And if individuals are martyred for Christ, they will receive crowns of glory.

"The end-times are already here; we see clearly the preparation of the world for the Antichrist," said Father Seraphim Rose. "Christians will be faced with an unprecedented trial of their faith and love for God. We will have to hide in the wilderness. . . . Of course, in the end they will find us even there. The purpose of hiding is not just for the preservation of our earthly life, but to gain time to strengthen our souls for the final trial. And this must begin even now. Let us therefore at least begin to struggle against the fetters of petty passions, and remember that our true home is not here, but in the heavens. Let us strive towards our heavenly homeland, as St. Herman [eighteenth-century Russian missionary to Alaska] used to say. . . . *Ad astera! Ad astera!* ['To the stars! To the stars!']"[24]

[1] Timothy (Bishop Kallistos) Ware, *The Orthodox Church*, p. 19.

[2] "Ad Martyras," in *The Ante-Nicene Fathers*, Vol. III, p. 694.

[3] *The Prologue from Ochrid*, Part 2, p. 326.

[4] "Apology," in *The Ante-Nicene Fathers*, Vol. III, p. 55.

[5] St. Nicholai Velimirovic, *The Prologue from Ochrid*, Part 4, p. 350.

[6] Paul Marshall Allen, *Vladimir Soloviev, Russian Mystic*, p. 134.

[7] *Unseen Warfare*, E. Kadloubovsky and G.E.H. Palmer, trans., p. 214.

[8] *The Orthodox Church*, p. 74.

[9] *The Meaning of Icons*, p. 180.

[10] Third Theological Oration, "On the Son," in *Nicene and Post-Nicene Fathers*, Vol. VII, p. 309.

[11] "Orthodox Worship: The Orthodox Worship of the Historic Church," *The Christian Activist*, Vol. 3, No. 1, Spring 1992, p. 36.

[12] *The Prologue from Ochrid*, Part 3, p. 6.

[13] "Preparing for the Underground Church," *Epiphany Journal*, Vol. 5, No. 4, Summer 1985, p. 46.

[14] *The Orthodox Church*, p. 26.

[15] Quoted in Christensen, *Not of This World*, p. 487.

[16] Quoted in *The Orthodox Church*, p. 19.

[17] *The Apocalypse of St. John*, pp. 136-137.

[18] *The Last Judgement*, p. 175.

[19] *A Ray of Light*, Archimandrite Panteleimon, comp., p. 87.

[20] *Not of This World*, p. 695.

[21] *Against False Union*, p. 65.

[22] Quoted in *Not of This World*, p. 281.

[23] "Preparing for the Underground Church," *Epiphany Journal*, Vol. 5, No. 4, Summer 1985, p. 48.

[24] *Not of This World*, p. 942.

Chapter 16

Armageddon

*Despise the sword, the fire, the cross, the wild
beasts, the torture; these surely are but trifling
sufferings to obtain a celestial glory and a divine
reward.*
— *Tertullian, "Ad Martyras"*

The "day of the Lord" is to be a time of the greatest
possible calamity. "Wail," cried Isaiah, "for the day of
the LORD is at hand! It will come as destruction from
the Almighty. Therefore all hands will be limp, every
man's heart will melt. . . . Behold, the day of the LORD
comes, cruel, with both wrath and fierce anger, to lay
the land desolate; and He will destroy its sinners from
it" (Isaiah 13:6, 7, 9).

Zechariah is more specific. There will be a great conflict between Jerusalem and other nations, which will be
fought in the valley of Megiddo. This area near Jerusalem
is known fearfully as Armageddon. "It shall be in that
day that I will seek to destroy all the nations that come
against Jerusalem. . . . In that day there shall be a great
mourning in Jerusalem, like the mourning at Hadad
Rimmon in the plain of Megiddo" (Zechariah 12:9, 11).

The day of the Lord is to be just that—the moment when Jesus Christ achieves uncontested victory over those who have opposed Him. "Behold, the day of the LORD is coming, and your spoil will be divided in your midst. For I will gather all the nations to battle against Jerusalem. . . . Then the LORD will go forth and fight against those nations" (Zechariah 14:1-3).

Jerusalem, the center of controversy for hundreds of years, will be the point of contention in history's greatest war. "Behold," cries Zechariah, "I will make Jerusalem a cup of drunkenness to all the surrounding peoples, when they lay siege against Judah and Jerusalem. And it shall happen in that day that I will make Jerusalem a very heavy stone for all peoples; all who would heave it away will surely be cut in pieces, though all nations of the earth are gathered against it" (Zechariah 12:2, 3).

Free from his thousand years of bondage, Satan will mount a great campaign to throw the world into utter confusion and despair, until the Lord triumphs. "Now when the thousand years have expired, Satan will be released from his prison and will go out to deceive the nations which are in the four corners of the earth, Gog and Magog, to gather them together to battle. . . . They went up on the breadth of the earth and surrounded the camp of the saints and the beloved city. And fire came down from God out of heaven and devoured them" (Revelation 20:7-9).

Blessed Augustine warned that Satan "shall burst forth from lurking hatred into open persecution. For this persecution, occurring while the final judgment is imminent, shall be the last which shall be endured by the holy Church throughout the world, the whole city of Christ being assailed by the whole city of the devil, as each exists on earth."[1]

The Last Battle

The Scriptures list a number of ancient nations, each stemming from a descendant of Noah, which are to come against Israel. Various commentators have associated these nations with modern countries or peoples, and some have confidently predicted the players and progression of the world's last, climactic battle. As the world's contemporary political landscape changes, however, these prognostications tend to ebb and flow (much like the calculated date of Christ's Return).

Daniel records the following scene: "At the time of the end the king of the South shall attack him; and the king of the North shall come against him like a whirlwind, with chariots, horsemen, and with many ships; and he shall enter the countries, overwhelm them, and pass through. . . . He shall have power over the treasures of gold and silver, and over all the precious things of Egypt; also the Libyans and Ethiopians shall follow at his heels. But news from the east and the north shall trouble him; therefore he shall go out with great fury to destroy and annihilate many. . . . Yet he shall come to his end, and no one will help him" (Daniel 11:40-45).

Whoever the earthly participants in this ghastly conflict may ultimately be, the real contestants are clearly Christ and Satan: "And I saw the beast, the kings of the earth, and their armies, gathered together to make war against Him [Christ] who sat on the horse and against His army" (Revelation 19:19).

The battle of Armageddon will represent the final, futile attempt by Satan to deny Christ what belongs to Him. Through immersing the world in war and misery, the evil one will exterminate whatever light of hope remains in those souls he has already marked. These are they who refused to repent, even in the face of God's plagues and punishments. To them is reserved the misery of total defeat.

"Another horse, fiery red, went out," wrote Saint John. "And it was granted to the one who sat on it to take peace from the earth, and that people should kill one another; and there was given to him a great sword" (Revelation 6:4).

Everything about this battle is extraordinary. Beyond the human warriors, there will be the working of unseen powers—voices, thunders and lightning. "And they gathered them together to the place called in Hebrew, Armageddon. Then the seventh angel poured out his bowl into the air, and a loud voice came out of the temple of heaven, from the throne, saying, 'It is done!' And there were noises and thunderings and lightnings; and there was a great earthquake, such a mighty and great earthquake as had not occurred since men were on the earth" (Revelation 16:16-18).

The earthquake will be the most powerful and damaging in human history. Saint Andrew of Caesarea cites other scriptural references to the heavens being shaken, which indicate a fundamental change in the earth: "The earthquake signifies a change in the existing world as the Apostle has said: *Yet once more I shake not the earth only, but also the heaven*—Heb. 12:2."

Dry Rivers

Two passages from the Book of Revelation indicate that the Euphrates River will be dried up and a great army from the East will advance across it. "Then the sixth angel poured out his bowl on the great river Euphrates, and its water was dried up, so that the way of the kings from the east might be prepared" (Revelation 16:12).

"And I heard a voice from the four horns of the golden altar which is before God, saying to the sixth angel who had the trumpet, 'Release the four angels who are bound at the great river Euphrates.' So the four angels, who had been prepared for the hour and day and month and year, were released to kill a third of mankind. Now the number of the army of the horsemen was two hundred million" (Revelation 9:13-16).

Casualties from this fighting will cause immense bloodshed. "So the angel thrust his sickle into the earth and gathered the vine of the earth, and threw it into the great winepress of the wrath of God. And the winepress was trampled outside the city, and blood came out of the winepress, up to the horses' bridles, for one thousand six hundred furlongs" (Revelation 14:19, 20).

As Archbishop Averky explained, "The hyperbolic expression used here by the holy seer of mysteries indicates that the defeat of the enemies of God will be so terrible that the blood will flow as if in rivers."[2] Carnage will be so extreme that bodies will lie rotting and unattended. All that was considered valuable in the world will seem as filth, and people will search everywhere for someplace to escape.

"There will be no place to run away or hide," cautions Saint Ephraim the Syrian, "for everything will be in confusion on sea and land. . . . The stench will hang over both sea and land; hunger, earthquakes, confusion, and calamities will abound. . . . All will regard as blessed those dead who were buried before such grief came to the earth. Gold and silver will be scattered over the streets, and no one will touch them for everything has become an abomination."[3]

Christians can be consoled in that this incredible war represents the final event before Christ's Return. With its conclusion, all "wars and rumors of wars" (Mark 13:7) will cease. The prayer which has issued passionately from so many hearts may then forever rest: "Deliver me from eternal fire, from wicked war and from hell" (Midnight Song to the Most Holy Mother of God).[4]

Archangel Michael Fights

Daniel predicts the Archangel Michael will lead Christ's troops to insure the battle's success: "At that time Michael shall stand up, the great prince who stands watch over the sons of your people; and there shall be a time of trouble, such as never was since there was a nation, even to that time. And at that time your people shall be delivered, every one who is found written in the book" (Daniel 12:1).

This is certainly fitting, for the ultimate conflict between good and evil on earth will be a reflection and completion of that primordial scene which occurred in heaven's realm. "And war broke out in heaven: Michael and his angels fought with the dragon; and the dragon and his angels fought, but they did not prevail, nor was a place found for them in heaven any longer. So the great dragon was cast out, that serpent of old, called the Devil and Satan, who deceives the whole world" (Revelation 12:7-9).

As Saint John promises, the dragon "did not prevail." As he was cast out of heaven to the earth, so will he be cast out of earth and into the lake of fire. His days of deception will at last end. On the other hand, those who have refused the mark of the beast, whose names are written in the Book of Life, will join in celebration at their Lord's momentous victory!

---

[1] *The City of God,* p. 729.
[2] *The Apocalypse of St. John,* p. 156.
[3] *A Ray of Light,* Archimandrite Panteleimon, comp., p. 94.
[4] *Prayer Book,* p. 19.

Chapter 17

The Second Coming

*When your sufferings shall have ended, your
righteousness shall go with you and the glory of
the Lord shall accompany you.*
        —*Saint John Maximovitch*

It may be that our Lord Jesus Christ was thinking
ahead to Antichrist when He said, "What profit is it to
a man if he gains the whole world, and loses his own
soul?" (Matthew 16:26). For, without a doubt, Antichrist will be the first and last human capable of gaining
the whole world. And the cost of this great acquisition
will be not only his own soul, but the souls of all people
who side with him.

Antichrist will become the undisputed secular and
religious leader, the so-called "god" of mankind. He
will "solve" many of life's problems, and those bearing
his mark will enjoy a brief period of pleasure and
prosperity.

At that time, all the troublesome Christians will be
either dead or in hiding. Worldly pursuits will preoc-
cupy the people of earth completely. Ignorant of the
disaster waiting in the wings, they will behave as though

they were immortal. "And as it was in the days of Noah," says the Gospel, "so it will be also in the days of the Son of Man: They ate, they drank, they married wives, they were given in marriage, until the day that Noah entered the ark, and the flood came and destroyed them all" (Luke 17:26, 27).

Metropolitan Anthony of Sourozh pointed out that the presence of Noah among his generation was both condemnation and salvation: "It was condemnation because the presence of *one* man who had remained faithful . . . was evidence that that was possible, and that those who were sinners, those who had rejected God . . . could have done likewise. . . . Yet it was also the salvation of his time, because he was the only one thanks to whom God looked with mercy upon man."[1]

So shall it be at the very end. The world will have reached its apex of carnality, its nadir of spirituality. Concerns of the flesh will be all-important. As Saint John Chrysostom noted, "Amid such evils they lived in luxury. . . . When Antichrist is come, the pursuit of unlawful pleasures shall be more eager among the transgressors. . . . But they that are held by the intoxication of wickedness shall not so much as perceive the dreadful nature of the things that are on the point of being done."[2]

He's Back!

God in His mercy and love will have sent many problems and scourges, as warnings to mankind that something is terribly wrong. Yet these will be explained away as natural disasters by scientists, medicated away by doctors, or just ignored. Finally, Christ will come.

All of sacred Scripture, all of world history, all of human experience, all of Satan's posturing—all testify through the ages that Christ is coming. Yet, to spiritually blind mankind, the day of the Lord will appear suddenly and unexpectedly, like "a thief in the night," as Saint Paul wrote. "For when they say, 'Peace and safety!' then sudden destruction comes upon them, as labor pains upon a pregnant woman. And they shall not escape" (1 Thessalonians 5:2, 3).

Up until the last moment, people will behave as though this world would last forever. "Likewise as it was also in the days of Lot: They [the Sodomites] ate, they drank, they bought, they sold, they planted, they built; but on the day that Lot went out of Sodom it rained fire and brimstone from heaven and destroyed them all. Even so will it be in the day when the Son of Man is revealed" (Luke 17:28-30).

In spite of the many admonitions, the world will never suspect its danger. Only those who treasure the words of the Lord Jesus Christ will be prepared: "But take heed to yourselves, lest your hearts be weighed down with carousing, drunkenness, and cares of this life, and that Day come on you unexpectedly. For it will come as a snare on all those who dwell on the face of the whole earth. Watch therefore, and pray always that you may be counted worthy to escape all these things that will come to pass, and to stand before the Son of Man" (Luke 21:34-36).

The Savior will not come from the earth or the sea, but from heaven, as the angels assured His Apostles so long ago: "Now I saw heaven opened, and behold, a white horse. And He who sat on him was called Faithful and True, and in righteousness He judges and makes war. His eyes were like a flame of fire, and on His head were many crowns. He had a name written that no one knew except Himself. He was clothed with a robe dipped in blood, and His name is called The Word of God" (Revelation 19:11-13).

In a blinding flash, the Lord will appear to a frightened world. He will be seen in the sky, that element which has so long been the realm of Satan. "For as the lightning comes from the east and flashes to the west, so also will the coming of the Son of Man be," wrote Saint Matthew. ". . . Then the sign of the Son of Man will appear in heaven, and then all the tribes of the earth will mourn, and they will see the Son of Man coming on the clouds of heaven with power and great glory. And He will send His angels with a great sound of a trumpet, and they will gather together His elect from the four winds, from one end of heaven to the other" (Matthew 24:27-31).

The sign of the Son of Man is, of course, the Cross. "The sign of the Cross shall be a terror to His foes," exclaims Saint Cyril of Jerusalem, "but joy to His friends who have believed in Him, or preached Him, or suffered for His sake."[3]

Saint John Maximovitch explained that Christ's appearance will bring all people to a recognition of the truth. "And the *Sign of the Son of God* will appear: the Sign of the Cross. The whole world, having willingly submitted to Antichrist, will weep. Everything is finished forever: Antichrist killed; the end of his kingdom of warfare with Christ; the end, and one is held accountable; one must answer to the true God."[4]

"At that time the whole earth will tremble," says the Apocalypse of Elijah. "The sun will be darkened. Peace will be removed from upon the earth and from under heaven. . . . The sinners will cry out on the earth, saying, 'What have you done to us, lawless one, by saying, "I am the Christ," when you are the lawless one? And you have no power to save yourself, much less to save us. You performed vain marvels before us until you had made us strangers to the Christ who created each one of us. Woe to us, because we listened to you! See, we are about to die in an evil manner and in affliction. . . . Now we will be destroyed by wrath, because we disobeyed God.' . . . Then the shameless one will weep . . . saying, 'Woe is me as well, because my time has passed!' "[5]

Unlike Antichrist, who will have had to deceive mankind, and to use all the modern technology available to advance his cause, Christ's Second Advent will cause an immediate spiritual shock throughout the world. "It will not be necessary or possible for persons to communicate news of the coming of the Son of God," wrote Saint Ignatius Brianchaninov. "He will appear suddenly . . . to all men and to all the earth at the same time."[6]

The Lord will descend to that very land from which he ascended before his disciples' astonished gaze so long before. He will repossess Jerusalem, Antichrist's capital, as her rightful Lord and King.

When he touches the Mount of Olives a tremendous earthquake will split the hill from east to west. "And in that day His [the Lord's] feet will stand on the Mount of Olives, which faces Jerusalem on the east. And the Mount of Olives shall be split in two, from east to west, making a very large valley" (Zechariah 14:4).

There will be a new heaven, a new earth, and a new humanity. Christ's Return will change *everything!*

New Heaven, New Earth

In Greece there is an ancient place called *Agion Oros*, the "Holy Mountain." Here monastic Christians have devoted themselves to God for hundreds of years. In Stavronikita, one of the peninsula's venerable monasteries, fifteenth-century icons painted by the Cretan master Theophanes present an unearthly portrait of sanctity.

The holy figures of Christ and His saints shown on these icons possess a remarkable luminosity, as though the light on their bodies is not reflected from an external source, but rather shines from within them. This illumination portrays the holiness to which Christians may attain.

The essence of divinity is light. As Saint John says, "God is light and in Him is no darkness at all" (1 John 1:5). Christ's Return at the end of the Great Tribulation will bathe the earth in divine light. As the evening stars fade from view at dawn, so shall all material sources of light pale beneath the brilliance of Christ's divine illumination. "There shall be no night there: They need no lamp nor light of the sun, for the Lord God gives them light" (Revelation 22:5).

Even the mighty sun will seem dark by comparison: "Immediately after the tribulation of those days the sun will be darkened, and the moon will not give its light; the stars will fall from heaven, and the powers of the heavens will be shaken" (Matthew 24:29-31). Referring to this, Saint John Chrysostom taught that the sun and stars are "not destroyed, but overcome by the light of His presence; and the stars shall fall, for what shall be the need of them thenceforth, there being no night?"[7]

The heavens which man watched for guidance during his long sojourn on earth will no longer be visible, for their Creator will again walk in brilliance with man. "For the stars of heaven and their constellations will not give their light," anticipated Isaiah. "The sun will be darkened in its going forth, and the moon will not cause its light to shine" (Isaiah 13:10).

In this new heaven and new earth, Satan will never enter. Death will not be known there, but only eternal life in God's righteousness. "We . . . look for new heavens and a new earth in which righteousness dwells" (2 Peter 3:13).

Uncreated Light, Immaterial Fire

The Lord's Transfiguration on Mount Tabor was also a preview of the glory of His Coming. The Gospel records that "His face shone like the sun, and His clothes became as white as the light" (Matthew 17:2). The *Festal Menaion* reading for Matins of the Transfiguration of our Lord includes these words: "Thou wast revealed as an immaterial fire that burns not the material substance of the body . . . showing the exchange mortal men will make with Thy glory at Thy second and fearful coming, O Saviour."[8]

The light of Christ will illumine those who are prepared for it, and burn those who are not, even as Saint Symeon's prayer before Holy Communion indicates: "O Thou Who givest me willingly Thy Flesh for food, Thou Who art fire, and burnest the unworthy, scorch me not, O my Maker, but rather pass through me for the integration of my members, into all my joints, my affections, and my heart. Burn up the thorns of all my sins."[9]

Prayers offered during Matins of the Holy Theophany of Our Lord characterize the last days themselves as a "fire," the final conflagration in which all unrighteousness is to be permanently consumed in the divine inferno. "Christ baptizes in the fire of the Last Day those who are disobedient and believe not that He is God: but through the Spirit and by the grace that comes through water He grants a new birth to all who acknowledge His divinity, delivering them from their faults."[10]

This blaze will penetrate into the depths of creation, removing all impurities forever: "But the heavens and the earth which are now preserved by the same word, are reserved for fire until the day of judgment and perdition of ungodly men. . . . But the day of the Lord will come as a thief in the night, in which the heavens will pass away with a great noise, and the elements will melt with fervent heat; both the earth and the works that are in it will be burned up" (2 Peter 3:7-13).

The Transformation

That creation which fell at Adam's sin will be restored to its pristine state of purity. Christ conquers more than Satan; He conquers death itself, which had ruled over all the natural world. As God had cursed the ground for Adam's sake (Genesis 3:17), so will He bless it and make it new. The earth which Saint John saw will be no more: "Now I saw a new heaven and a new earth, for the first heaven and the first earth had passed away" (Revelation 21:1).

The "end of this world" does not produce obliteration (except of evil), but rather restoration and renewal. "For this world shall pass away by transmutation, not by absolute destruction," wrote Blessed Augustine. "And therefore the apostle says, 'For the figure of this world passeth away' (1 Cor. 7:31). The figure, therefore, passes away, not the nature."[11]

"Thus the whole creation, after it will be renewed and become spiritual, will become a dwelling which is immaterial, incorruptible, unchanging, and eternal," added Saint Symeon. "The heaven will become incomparably more brilliant and bright than it appears now; it will become completely new. The earth will receive a new, unutterable beauty, being clothed in many-formed, unfading flowers, bright and spiritual. . . . The whole world will become more perfect than any word can describe."[12]

The creatures of God's world will also be restored to their original purity, which was lost following Adam's Fall. By the triumph of Jesus Christ, "the creation itself also will be delivered from the bondage of corruption into the glorious liberty of the children of God. For we know that the whole creation groans and labors with birth pangs together until now" (Romans 8:21, 22).

The ultimate meaning of the end times is transformation, according to Saint John Maximovitch. " 'The end of the world' signifies not the annihilation of the world, but its transformation. Everything will be transformed suddenly, in the twinkling of an eye. The dead will rise in new bodies: their own, but renewed, just as the Saviour rose in His own body and on it were traces of wounds from the nails and spear, yet it possessed new faculties, and in this sense it was a new body."[13]

Along with the changing of earth and heaven, there will occur a changing of men. Those who are Christian, whether living or dead, will be transformed. The light of Christ will instantly cleanse them of mortality. "We shall not all sleep, but we shall all be changed—in a moment, in the twinkling of an eye, at the last trumpet," wrote Saint Paul. "For the trumpet will sound, and the dead will be raised incorruptible, and we shall be changed" (1 Corinthians 15:51, 52).

Isaiah prophesied that even the dead would return

to life to stand before God. "Your dead shall live; together with my dead body they shall arise" (Isaiah 26:19).

The hallowed dead, having patiently waited in their graves during the Lord's absence, will be the first to celebrate His Return. "For this we say to you by the word of the Lord, that we who are alive and remain until the coming of the Lord will by no means precede those who are asleep. For the Lord Himself will descend from heaven with a shout, with the voice of an archangel, and with the trumpet of God. And the dead in Christ will rise first. Then we who are alive and remain shall be caught up together with them in the clouds to meet the Lord in the air. And thus we shall always be with the Lord" (1 Thessalonians 4:15-17).

The image of the new earth, or the "world to come," is Christ Himself. This He revealed in that His resurrected body was spiritual while still being physical. Such will the new earth be. Father Michael Oleksa writes, "Then He appeared suddenly in the upper room, 'the doors being shut,' and His disciples were at first afraid that it was only a ghost that they saw. The Lord however insisted that it was really He Himself and not a ghost, for 'a spirit does not have flesh and bones as you see me have.' Obviously Christ was not the same as He had been. His friends did not immediately recognize Him on the road to Emmaus. He could appear and disappear unexpectedly, yet He ate with the apostles and allowed them to touch Him. Thus, the risen Lord, as the 'first fruits of those who are asleep,' reveals that

His kingdom is not totally 'spiritualized' to the extent that the physical dimension is eliminated. Of course, the material body is radically transformed, or rather restored to its original perfection, but it is not destroyed. It is the resurrection, perhaps even more than the nativity, that justifies the Orthodox belief that the creation will share in the transfiguration of the universe, that the physical world participates in eternity and has an essential function to serve both now and in the kingdom."[14]

[1] *Meditations,* B#28A, pp. 2-4, as quoted in *The Bible and the Holy Fathers,* Johanna Manley, ed., p. 709.

[2] "Homilies on the Gospel of St. Matthew," Homily LXXVII, in *Nicene and Post-Nicene Fathers,* Vol. X, p. 464.

[3] "Catechetical Lectures," Lecture XV, Part 22, in *Nicene and Post-Nicene Fathers,* Vol. VII, p. 111.

[4] *The Last Judgement,* p. 177.

[5] "Dies Irae," *Epiphany Journal,* Winter 1983, pp. 64-65.

[6] "On the Kingdom of God," *Epiphany Journal,* Vol. 9, No. 1, Fall 1988, p. 57.

[7] "Homilies on the Gospel of St. Matthew," Homily LXXVI, in *Nicene and Post-Nicene Fathers,* Vol. X, p. 459.

[8] *Festal Menaion,* Archimandrite Kallistos Ware and Mother Mary, trans., pp. 478, 486.

[9] *Prayer Book,* pp. 351-352.

[10] *Festal Menaion,* pp. 373-374.

[11] *The City of God,* p. 732.

[12] *The First-Created Man,* p. 104.

[13] *The Last Judgement,* pp. 177-178.

[14] "Icons and the Cosmos," *Epiphany Journal,* Vol. 8, No. 4, Summer 1988, p. 72.

Chapter 18

The Last Judgment

*We will be able, with good hope and spiritual
intimation of mercy and salvation, to stand
before the impartial Judge, Who is to pronounce
the verdict which will determine our lot for
eternity.*

—*Saint Ignatius Brianchaninov*

At the Last Judgment, each soul will receive from
God the reward of his good or evil deeds. This will be
an occasion of the greatest joy for all true believers.
"Awake and sing, you who dwell in dust. . . . For
behold, the LORD comes out of His place to punish the
inhabitants of the earth for their iniquity" (Isaiah
26:19-21).

Saint Ephraim the Syrian describes the scene thus:
"The graves will open, and in the twinkling of an eye all
of the tribes will be awakened and will look upon the
holy greatness of the Bridegroom. Great multitudes of
Angels and Archangels, countless armies, will rejoice
with great joy; the saints, the righteous, and all who had
not accepted the seal of the ungodly serpent, will
rejoice. . . . All who had been hiding in caves, will

rejoice together with the Bridegroom in the eternal and heavenly mansions with all the saints unto the ages of ages."[1]

The Lord's Judgment will be impartial and just, based on everything a person thought, did and said, consciously or unconsciously, from birth till death. "And I saw the dead, small and great, standing before God, and books were opened. And another book was opened, which is the Book of Life. And the dead were judged according to their works, by the things which were written in the books" (Revelation 20:12). God will also judge those who have survived until the Second Coming, as the Nicene Creed says: "He is coming again with glory to judge the living and the dead; and His kingdom will have no end."

The Judgment, explained Blessed Augustine, is "a certain divine power, by which it shall be brought about that every one shall recall to memory all his own works, whether good or evil, and shall mentally survey them with a marvellous rapidity, so that this knowledge will either accuse or excuse conscience, and thus all and each shall be simultaneously judged. . . . For it is not that God is ignorant, and reads in the book to inform Himself, but rather His infallible prescience is the book of life in which they are written."[2]

"With what eyes then shall we behold Christ?" asks Saint John Chrysostom. "For if any one could not bear to see his father, when conscious to himself that he had sinned against him, upon Him who infinitely exceeds a father in forbearance how shall we then look? how shall we bear it? For indeed we shall stand at Christ's judgment-seat, and there will be a strict inquiry into all things."[3]

Each person's lifetime of choices for or against God will culminate in a final determination, as Saint Ephraim the Syrian wrote: "All of humanity will find itself between the kingdom and condemnation, between life and death, between joy and necessity, and all will stand before the judgement seat, looking downwards and not daring to raise up their eyes. All will be interrogated and strictly tried, especially we who have lived in carelessness, and seeing all this will start thinking over all their deeds. Each person will see his own deeds, bad and good. All those whose deeds are good will joyfully draw near to the judgement seat in the hope of obtaining a crown. If anyone who has serious sins on his conscience leaves this life without repenting, he will become sick at heart when he sees his sins standing before him, accusing him and condemning him, and he will say, 'Why did I the poor one not struggle with them, but wasted time playing games and so became myself a plaything? . . . Why did I not repent before Him who takes away the sin of the world, but spent my years in delusion? . . . What am I to do? The time for repentance has passed by'."[4]

The End of Death

At Christ's Return, death will be no more. "Then comes the end, when He delivers the kingdom to God the Father, when He puts an end to all rule and all authority and power. For He must reign till He has put all enemies under His feet. The last enemy that will be destroyed is death" (1 Corinthians 15:24-26).

The loving Father of mankind will heal His children of all their wounds and sorrows, the greatest of which was dying. "And God will wipe away every tear from their eyes; there shall be no more death, nor sorrow, nor crying. There shall be no more pain, for the former things have passed away" (Revelation 21:4). In the end, death itself is punished along with those evil ones who first brought it upon humanity, for Revelation says, "Then Death and Hades were cast into the lake of fire" (Revelation 20:14).

God is not God of the dead, but of the living, and eternal life is not a reward, but a fact. The Judgment is not to determine whether one lives or dies, but whether one will live eternally in heaven or in hell. "The hour is coming in which all who are in the graves will hear His voice and come forth—those who have done good, to the resurrection of life, and those who have done evil, to the resurrection of condemnation" (John 5:28, 29).

The Judge

In a very real sense, each person is his own first judge. For the life that a person has led will incline either toward or away from Christ. The divine light of the Lord will be as a burning fire to some, and as a soothing glow to others. Saint John Maximovitch writes, "Fire will be kindled within a man: seeing the Cross, some will rejoice, but others will fall into confusion, terror, and despair. Thus will men be divided instantly. The very state of a man's soul casts him to one side or the other, to right or to left."[5]

For the many sinners who have submitted themselves to Antichrist and who carry the mark of the beast, the Judgment of the Lord will be a terrifying experience in which all that they are (except the soul itself) and have done is destroyed. " 'For behold, the day is coming, burning like an oven, and all the proud, yes, all who do wickedly will be stubble. And the day which is coming shall burn them up,' says the LORD of hosts, 'that will leave them neither root nor branch' " (Malachi 4:1).

Those who have rejected Christ will meet Reality much as a fish meets dry land—without any capacity to function in that environment. "They enter into eternity in no way prepared for it, in no way acquainted with it," declared Saint Ignatius Brianchaninov. "This is not enough: they enter into it having assimilated a temperament entirely at enmity with its spiritual blessings, with the happiness which belongs to it there."[6]

At the Judgment, no further deception, either of oneself or others, is possible. "Everything becomes clear to all and to oneself," wrote Saint John Maximovitch. "And some will go to joy, while others—to horror.

"When 'the books are opened,' it will become clear that the roots of all vices lie in the human soul. Here is a drunkard or a lecher: when the body has died, some may think that sin is dead too. No! There was an inclination to sin in the soul, and that sin was sweet to the soul, and if the soul has not repented of the sin and has not freed itself from it, it will come to the Last Judgement also with the same desire for sin. It will never satisfy that desire and in that soul there will be the suffering of hatred. It will accuse everyone and everything in its tortured condition, it will hate everyone and everything. 'There will be gnashing of teeth' of powerless malice and the unquenchable fire of hatred.

"A 'fiery gehenna'—such is the inner fire. 'Here there will be wailing and gnashing of teeth.' Such is the state of hell."[7]

The Sheep and the Goats

The Lord's Judgment shall separate saints from sinners permanently, as Saint Ephraim explains: "After each one has been tried before men, and all dominions and powers have been abolished and all God's enemies have been placed under His feet; then at last, as the Lord said, 'He shall separate them one from another, as a shepherd divideth his sheep from the goats: and He shall set the sheep on His right hand, but the goats on the left' (Mt. 25:32-33). . . . Then parents will be separated from children, fathers from sons, mothers from daughters, friends and relatives from each other. Then false spouses who have not kept their bed undefiled will be separated. But I will pass by much in silence in my description; for fear restrains me from telling about this."[8]

"After the final and decisive sentence has been

passed at the universal judgement," reads *Apostasy and Antichrist,* "the eternal blessedness of the righteous in the kingdom of heaven will begin, as well as the eternal torments of sinners in hell (Lk. 16:23), a place of all woes, sufferings and punishments, where there is only disorder, terror and confusion, where there is no joy of any kind nor any hope whatever of any alleviation (Mk. 9:44, 46-48). Eternal separation from God and deprivation of all God's gifts, tormenting pangs of conscience, eternal disgrace and shame, reproaches, mockery and cursing from those who had been drawn into sin by the condemned; the onslaught of demons, living together with them and with all the condemned—will bring about that 'gnashing of teeth' (Mt. 22:13) which the Saviour mentions. For the righteous, on the contrary, a great reward is prepared. They will be led into the most perfect and beautiful place, which in Holy Scripture is called paradise (Lk. 23:43), heaven (Mt. 6:9), and the heavenly kingdom (Mt. 5:3). Here the righteous will enjoy the direct vision of God, seeing Him 'face to face' (1 Cor. 13:12). This means that the glory and majesty of the Lord will become accessible for the righteous. . . . In this contemplation they will find complete satisfaction for the mind, will and heart, and an inexhaustible source of eternal enjoyment and blessedness; eternal joy and eternal gladness will be their heritage."[9]

To those who have been judged worthy of that blessed life in heaven, the Lord will say, "Come, you blessed of My Father, inherit the kingdom prepared for you from the foundation of the world" (Matthew 25:34).

To those who are not judged to be worthy of heaven, the Lord will say, "Depart from Me, you who practice lawlessness!" (Matthew 7:23). And this is fitting, for as Father Seraphim Rose noted, "Nothing less than Hell is worthy of man, if he be not worthy of Heaven."[10]

Fate of the "Unholy Trinity"

"But when this Antichrist shall have devastated all things in this world," wrote Saint Irenaeus (A.D. 185), "he will reign for three years and six months, and sit in the temple at Jerusalem; and then the Lord will come from heaven in the clouds, in the glory of the Father, sending this man and those who follow him into the lake of fire."[11]

Saint Ephraim adds, "The tormentor, with all of the demons bound by angels, all who received the seal, all the ungodly and sinners, will be bound and brought to judgment. The King will issue a sentence of eternal condemnation in unquenchable fire."[12]

The fate of the Antichrist and his cronies is preordained; God's Judgment is already given. They are to suffer forever in a pool of fire: "Then the beast was captured, and with him the false prophet who worked signs in his presence, by which he deceived those who received the mark of the beast and those who worshiped his image. These two were cast alive into the lake of fire burning with brimstone" (Revelation 19:20).

Satan will also join his servants in hell. His "little season" ended, the son of perdition, beyond the pale of redemption, will remain constantly agonized by the love of God which he has willfully rejected. "The devil, who deceived them, was cast into the lake of fire and brimstone where the beast and the false prophet are. And they will be tormented day and night forever and ever" (Revelation 20:10).

But why forever? In all of eternity is there no chance that Satan and his minions will repent? Impossible, declared Memesius of Emesa in the fourth century: "As for angels, seeing there is no compulsion drawing them to sin, and that they are by nature exempt from bodily passions, needs, and pleasures, there is plain reason why they cannot claim pardon by repenting."[13]

Further clarifying this point, Saint Theophan the Recluse wrote, "The righteous will go into eternal life, but the satanized sinners into eternal torments, in communion with demons. Will these torments end? If satanism and becoming like satan should end, then the torments also can end. But is there an end to satanism and becoming like satan? . . . No conjectures can show the possibility of the end of satanism. What did satan not see after his fall! How much of the powers of God was revealed! How he himself was struck by the power of the Lord's Cross! How up to now all his cunningness and malice are defeated by this power! But still he is incorrigible, he constantly opposes; and the farther he goes, the more stubborn he becomes. No, there is no hope at all for him to be corrected! And if there is no hope for him, then there is no hope either for men who become satanized by his influence. This means that there must be hell with eternal torments."[14]

[1] *A Ray of Light,* Archimandrite Panteleimon, comp., p. 96.

[2] *The City of God,* pp. 733, 735.

[3] "Homilies on the Gospel of St. Matthew," Homily LXXVI, in *Nicene and Post-Nicene Fathers,* Vol. X, p. 461.

[4] "Sermon on the Honourable and Life-Creating Cross and on the Second Coming," as quoted in *Apostasy and Antichrist,* Puhalo & Novakshonoff, trans., pp. 43-44.

[5] *The Last Judgement,* p. 178.

[6] "On the Kingdom of God," *Epiphany Journal,* Vol. 9, No. 1, Fall 1988, p. 56.

[7] *The Last Judgement,* p. 178.

[8] "Sermon on the Honourable and Life-Creating Cross and on the Second Coming," as quoted in *Apostasy and Antichrist,* p. 44.

[9] *Apostasy and Antichrist,* pp. 44-45.

[10] "Man Against God," *The Orthodox Word,* Vol. 29, Nos. 5-6 (172-3), Sept.-Dec. 1993, p. 99.

[11] *Against Heresies,* Book V, ch. 30, par. 4, in *The Ante-Nicene Fathers,* Vol. I, p. 560.

[12] *A Ray of Light,* p. 96.

[13] *Of the Nature of Man,* as quoted in *The World Treasury of Religious Quotations,* Ralph L. Woods, ed., p. 18.

[14] As quoted in Pomazansky, *Orthodox Dogmatic Theology,* p. 351.

The Eleventh Hour

*The primary key to our being or non-being
resides in each individual human heart, in the
heart's preference for specific good or evil.*
—*Alexander Solzhenitsyn*

One of the temptations which assails those who recognize the signs of the end times is faintheartedness. In a society racked by and reeking of evil, what can possibly be done? It is easy to throw up one's hands and surrender.

True, the world is doomed—its collision course with catastrophe cannot be diverted. Because Satan is its ruler, the world will experience the same fate as the strong man who "owns" it (see Matthew 12:29; John 14:30).

Satan does *not* own human souls, however. "Behold, all souls are Mine," declares our heavenly Father (Ezekiel 18:4), who is a jealous God. Because God loves mankind and Christ died for mankind, envious Satan wants to steal human souls away—to destroy them.

And because God gave his beloved mankind free will, Satan will unfortunately achieve some success;

each person must ultimately, voluntarily and permanently choose between good and evil. Thus, in the end, every soul ever born will belong to either Christ or Antichrist.

This is the great question of the last days. Satan has already led into captivity a third of the original angelic host. But what percentage of mankind will he claim? Is it to be one-half? "Two men will be in the field: the one will be taken and the other left" (Luke 17:36). "Then the kingdom of heaven shall be likened to ten virgins who took their lamps and went out to meet the bridegroom. Now five of them were wise, and five were foolish" (Matthew 25:1, 2).

Is it to be two-thirds? " 'And it shall come to pass in all the land,' says the LORD, 'that two-thirds in it shall be cut off and die, but one-third shall be left in it: I will bring the one-third through the fire. . . . I will say, "This is My people"; and each one will say, "The LORD is my God" ' " (Zechariah 13:8, 9).

This great question can only be answered personally, for each of us must "choose . . . this day whom you will serve" (Joshua 24:15). The world in the last days will see intense political, social, economic and religious upheavals—in fact, every arena of human experience will be uprooted. Mankind will experience catastrophes in all directions, yet these external cataclysms are merely diversions by the enemy, distractions from the true battleground: the heart of man.

As Vladimir Soloviev's mother often told him, quoting her ancestor, the holy pilgrim Grigory Skovoroda,

"The spiritual heart encompasses and includes everything. . . . It is the real man."[1] Though the earth itself shakes and trembles, it is only here, in man's own heart, that the great contest will be decided—that Christ's Kingdom will be won or lost.

God does not force man to choose good, but has made him capable of doing so, and given His own Son as proof that this is possible. It is this freedom of which Dostoevsky's Grand Inquisitor complains (as though to Christ Himself), saying God created man to "decide with a free heart what is good and what is evil, with only your image before him to guide him."[2]

Ultimately, the great scales of the Last Judgment are hung from man's very heartstrings; with each inclination toward virtue or vice he tips them to the right or left, throughout his whole life. "The line separating good and evil passes not through states, nor between classes," wrote novelist Alexander Solzhenitsyn, who himself gained faith in Christ by suffering under communist atheism, "nor between political parties either—but right through every human heart—and through all human hearts. . . . And even within hearts overwhelmed by evil, one small bridgehead of good is retained. And even in the best of all hearts, there remains . . . an unuprooted small corner of evil."[3]

As only the heart can choose Christ, only the heart can recognize its Lord. And only the humble heart which loves its Lord can recognize the Lord's great opponent. Only when the heart belongs firmly to Christ, when "the kingdom of God is within" (Luke

17:21), is there any hope at all of resisting Antichrist.

"He who has received within himself the kingdom of God can have a clear understanding concerning the second coming of the God-man," preached Saint Ignatius Brianchaninov. "He can recognize and escape the antichrist or oppose him. He who has not received within himself the kingdom of God cannot recognize the antichrist. He is absolutely sure to become, in a way incomprehensible to himself, his follower."[4]

Knowing this, each struggling Christian must be bold, holding fast to his Savior, to the Faith of the undivided Church, and rejecting any inclination to compromise out of faintheartedness.

"So you must never be afraid," believers are counseled in *Unseen Warfare*, "if you are troubled by a flood of thoughts, that the enemy is too strong against you, that his attacks are never ending, that the war will last for your lifetime, and that you cannot avoid incessant downfalls of all kinds. Know that our enemies, with all their wiles, are in the hands of our divine Commander, our Lord Jesus Christ, for Whose honour and glory you are waging war. Since He Himself leads you into battle, He will certainly not suffer your enemies to use violence against you and overcome you, if you do not yourself cross over to their side with your will. He will Himself fight for you and will deliver your enemies into your hands, when He wills and as He wills, as it is written: 'The Lord thy God walketh in the midst of thy camp, to deliver thee, and to give up thine enemies before thee' (Deut. xxiii.14)."[5]

Go into the Vineyard

In the end times Jesus offers to mankind a final wake-up call. Though a person may have wasted the time which should have been used to repent, or may have fallen into grievous sins, he is given a last chance to "clean up his act," to serve Christ and thus receive the same reward of salvation as others who have labored all along for the Lord.

The Gospel describes the Kingdom of heaven in terms of a man looking for workers: "And about the eleventh hour he went out and found others standing idle, and said to them, 'Why have you been standing here idle all day?' They said to him, 'Because no one hired us.' He said to them, 'You also go into the vineyard, and whatever is right you will receive' " (Matthew 20:6, 7).

Go into the vineyard of the heart, and labor there, says the Lord. Struggle to root out vice, and to acquire virtue. Confess your sins and strive to pray without ceasing. This is the work every Christian is called to, which is all that he can do, and at the same time is more than he can do. "I fear, O Lord, Thy Judgment and the endless torments, yet I cease not to do evil," lamented Saint John of Damascus.[6]

Even when Christians remind themselves that Christ's Return is imminent, and that the Judge is preparing to open His books—still they are drawn daily into temptations which threaten their faith or throw them into faintheartedness. "For both the time is short," preached Saint John Chrysostom, "and the labor small, and yet we faint and are supine. Thou strivest on earth, and the crown is in Heaven; thou art punished of men, and art honored of God; the race is for two days, and the reward for endless ages."[7]

The Fathers teach that wakefulness and watchfulness are the best antidotes for such spiritual malaise. For only malaise can explain the complacency of those who are careless when their life—especially their eternal life—is in jeopardy. "Every one should dwell attentively on the holy pronouncements of the Lord and Saviour," cautioned Saint Ephraim the Syrian, "for He, because of extreme need and grief, desires to shorten the time of woe, admonishing us and saying: . . . *Watch ye, and pray always, that ye may be accounted worthy to escape these woes, and to stand before the Son of Man* (Luke 21:36); for the time is near. All of us are subject to this grief, but do not despair. Worshipping God day and night, let us sinners unceasingly ask in tears and prayer, that we be saved.

"Whoever has contrition and tears should entreat the Lord in prayer that he escape from such great grief which will visit the earth, and that he should not see the beast himself, nor the terrors, quakes, hunger, and deaths which will occur all over the world. A steadfast soul is needed in order to be capable of directing one's life amid these temptations. If any person proves to be even slightly careless, he will be more easily captivated and overcome by the signs of the evil and crafty serpent. Such a one will find no pardon at the judgment, for he himself voluntarily believed the tormentor. We shall need many tears and prayers, O beloved, for some of us to firmly withstand these temptations. The beast will produce many visions; for he fights against God, and desires the destruction of everyone."[8]

The Last Christians

The Christians of this generation may be history's most disadvantaged. Living in perhaps the worst spiritual circumstances of all time, they are surrounded by a world which rejects Truth and opposes God. Authentic spiritual guidance, in this age which is nearly bereft of godly elders, is extremely difficult to find. Even with the great works of the Apostles and the ascetic achievements of the Holy Fathers as examples, today's believers are plagued with inertia and feebleness.

Yet it may be that the constant, humbling struggles, in which one's sinfulness before God shows so clearly, are the most providential antidotes to the satanic spirit of this age. For it is certain that no human strength, whether physical, emotional or mental, can resist Antichrist. And the last Christians know, if they are honest with themselves, that they are not equal to the task ahead.

Still, it is these last Christians, with all their imperfections and liabilities, who are called to "persevere until the end." Though weaker and less capable than those able martyrs and confessors who have gone before, it is they who must uphold the "shield of faith" (Ephesians 6:16) which, being tiny as a mustard seed, will nevertheless move great mountains. And God promises, "He who overcomes shall inherit all things, and I will be his God and he shall be My son" (Revelation 21:7).

Christ loves His last Christians; He calls them His "elect" and treasures them as the means of frustrating His evil adversary. For God in His wisdom "has chosen the weak things of the world to put to shame the things which are mighty" (1 Corinthians 1:27). As He has done so many times before, with Moses, Gideon, Saint Paul and others—mere mortals all—God accepts the disadvantage, knowing that His "strength is made perfect in weakness" (2 Corinthians 12:9).

Prayer

May the last Christians be at peace with the life of struggle which God has granted them. May they be grateful for every opportunity to join their Lord in suffering, for He has promised, "If they persecuted Me, they will also persecute you" (John 15:20). May they prepare for ever greater trials, and be eager to boldly declare the True Faith. May they look with hope to the coming of Christ, knowing that "the sufferings of this present time are not worthy to be compared with the glory which shall be revealed in us" (Romans 8:18). May they love God, and love those who love God. May they be worthy of heaven!

For You are holy, O our God, and we send up glory to You, to the Father and to the Son, and to the Holy Spirit, now and ever and unto the ages of ages. Amen.

Even so, Lord Jesus Christ, come quickly!

[1] Paul Marshall Allen, *Vladimir Soloviev, Russian Mystic*, p. 13.

[2] *The Brothers Karamazov*, Vol. 1, p. 293.

[3] *The Gulag Archipelago Two*, p. 615.

[4] "On the Kingdom of God," *Epiphany Journal*, Vol. 9, No. 1, Fall 1988, p. 53.

[5] *Unseen Warfare*, E. Kadloubovsky and G.E.H. Palmer, trans., p. 111.

[6] *Prayer Book*, p. 55.

[7] "Homilies on the Gospel of St. Matthew," Homily LXXVI, in *Nicene and Post-Nicene Fathers*, Vol. X, p. 460.

[8] *A Ray of Light*, Archimandrite Panteleimon, comp., p. 88.

List of References

"Developing Countries Fight Population Schemes," *Catholic Twin Circle,* Vol. 28, No. 29, July 19, 1992

"Dies Irae," *Epiphany Journal,* Vol. 3, No. 2, Winter 1983

"Letter from Russia," *Orthodox America,* Vol. XIII, No. 8, May-June 1993

Little Russian Philokalia, Vol. 1: St. Seraphim of Sarov, Platina, CA: St. Herman of Alaska Press, 1991

Prayer Book, Jordanville, NY: Holy Trinity Monastery, 1979

"The Prophetic Gift: Schema-Archimandrite Lavrenty of the Chernigov-Trinity Convent," *Orthodox America,* October 1989

Utne Reader, January-February 1995

Paul Marshall Allen, *Vladimir Soloviev, Russian Mystic,* Blauvelt, NY: Steinerbooks, 1978

I.M. Andreyev, *Russia's Catacomb Saints: Lives of the New Martyrs,* Platina, CA: St. Herman of Alaska Press, 1982

St. Augustine, *The City of God,* translated by Marcus Dods, New York: Modern Library, 1950

Archbishop Averky, *The Apocalypse of St. John: An Orthodox Commentary,* Platina, CA: Valaam Society of America, 1985

Archbishop Averky, *Stand Fast in the Truth,* compiled by Fr. Demetrios Serfes, translated from the Russian by Father Seraphim Johnson, Mt. Holy Springs, PA: Russian Orthodox Church Abroad

Fr. Michael Azkoul, *Anti-Christianity: The New Atheism,* Montreal: Monastery Press, 1981

Fr. Michael Azkoul, *Sacred Monarchy and the Modern Secular State,* Montreal: Monastery Press, 1984

St. Basil the Great, *On the Holy Spirit,* Crestwood, NY: St. Vladimir's Seminary Press, 1980

St. Ignatius Brianchaninov, *The Arena,* Jordanville, NY: Holy Trinity Monastery, 1983

St. Ignatius Brianchaninov, "On Miracles and Signs," *Orthodox Life,* Vol. 45, No. 2, March-April 1995

St. Ignatius Brianchaninov, "On the Kingdom of God," *Epiphany Journal,* Vol. 9, No. 1, Fall 1988

Monk Damascene Christensen, *Not of This World: The Life and Teaching of Fr. Seraphim Rose*, Forestville, CA: Fr. Seraphim Rose Foundation, 1993

Archimandrite Constantine of Holy Trinity Monastery, *Ecumenism, Communism and Apostasy: The Spiritual State of the Contemporary World*, Liberty, TN: St. John of Kronstadt Press

James Dale Davidson, *Forecasts & Forewarnings,* Baltimore, MD: Agora Financial Publishing, January 2, 1995

Archimandrite Dimitri, *Myrrhbearers,* Vol. II, No. 3, Autumn 1994

Fyodor Dostoevsky, *The Brothers Karamazov,* New York: Penguin Classics, 1972

Fyodor Dostoevsky, *The Grand Inquisitor,* New York: Ungar, 1956

Romano Guardini, *The Lord,* Chicago: Henry Regnery Company, 1954

Thomas Ice and Randall Price, *Ready to Rebuild,* Eugene, OR: Harvest House, 1992

Grant R. Jeffrey, *Armageddon: Appointment with Destiny,* New York: Bantam Books, 1990

E. Kadloubovsky and G.E.H. Palmer, translators, *Unseen Warfare,* Crestwood, NY: St. Vladimir's Seminary Press, 1978

Alexander Kalomiros, *Against False Union*, Seattle, WA: St. Nectarios Press, 1990

R. Monk Zachariah Liebmann, "The Life of Tsar-Martyr Nicholas II," *The Orthodox Word,* Vol. 26, No. 4 (153), July-August 1990

Niccolò Machiavelli, *The Prince,* New York: Mentor Books, 1952

Johanna Manley, editor, *The Bible and the Holy Fathers,* Menlo Park, CA: Monastery Press, 1990

St. John Maximovitch, *The Last Judgement,* Platina, CA: St. Herman of Alaska Press

St. John Maximovitch, *A New Age of Martyrs and Catacombs,* Platina, CA: St. Herman of Alaska Press

St. John Maximovitch, *Tsar-Martyr Nicholas II*, Platina, CA: St. Herman of Alaska Press, 1963

Bernard McGinn, translator and editor, *Apocalyptic Spirituality*, New York: Paulist Press, 1979

Vincent P. Miceli, S.J., *The Antichrist,* Harrison, NY: Roman Catholic Books, 1981

Czeslaw Milosz, "Science Fiction and the Coming of Antichrist," *Epiphany Journal*, Vol. 6, No. 4, Summer 1986

Archpriest Boris Molchanoff, *Antichrist,* Liberty, TN: St. John of Kronstadt Press, 1980

Thomas Molnar, *Utopia: The Perennial Heresy*, Lanham, MD: University Press of America, 1990

Bishop Nektary, "The Mystical Meaning of the Tsar's Martyrdom," *The Orthodox Word*, Vol. 24, Nos. 5-6 (142-143), September-December 1988

Friedrich Nietzsche, *The Complete Works of Friedrich Nietzsche*, New York: Russell & Russell, 1964

Fr. Michael Oleksa, "Icons and the Cosmos," *Epiphany Journal*, Vol. 8, No. 4, Summer 1988

Leonid Ouspensky, *The Meaning of Icons*, Crestwood, NY: St. Vladimir's Seminary Press, 1982

Archimandrite Panteleimon, compiler, *A Ray of Light: Instructions in Piety and the State of the World at the End of Time*, translated by Michael Hilko, Jordanville, NY: Holy Trinity Monastery, 1991

Jaroslav Pelikan, *The Christian Tradition*, Vol. 1: *The Emergence of the Catholic Tradition*, Chicago: The University of Chicago Press, 1971

Arthur W. Pink, *The Antichrist*, Grand Rapids, MI: Kregel Publications, 1988

Protopresbyter Michael Pomazansky, *Orthodox Dogmatic Theology*, Platina, CA: St. Herman of Alaska Press, 1984

Deacon Lev Puhalo and Vasili Novakshonoff, translators, *Apostasy and Antichrist*, Jordanville, NY: Holy Trinity Monastery, 1978

Alexander Roberts and James Donaldson, editors, *The Ante-Nicene Fathers*, Grand Rapids, MI: Wm. B. Eerdmans Publishing Co., 1975-1979

Eugene (Fr. Seraphim) Rose, "Christian Realism and Worldly Idealism," *The Orthodox Word*, Vol. 22, No. 3 (128), May-June 1986

Eugene (Fr. Seraphim) Rose, *Nihilism: The Root of the Revolution of the Modern Age*, Forestville, CA: Fr. Seraphim Rose Foundation, 1994

Fr. Seraphim Rose, *Heavenly Realm*, Platina, CA: St. Herman of Alaska Press, 1984

Fr. Seraphim Rose, "Man Against God," *The Orthodox Word*, Vol. 29, Nos. 5-6 (172-3), September-December 1993

Philip Schaff and Henry Wace, editors, *A Select Library of Nicene and Post-Nicene Fathers of the Christian Church*, Grand Rapids, MI: Wm. B. Eerdmans Publishing Co., 1978

C.I. Scofield, editor, *Holy Bible*, New York: Oxford University Press, 1967

William Shakespeare, *The Complete Works of Shakespeare*, W.J. Craig, editor, London: Oxford University Press, 1928

Alexander Solzhenitsyn, *The Gulag Archipelago Two*, New York: Harper and Row, 1975

St. Symeon the New Theologian, *The First-Created Man,* Platina, CA: St. Herman of Alaska Press, 1994

William Irwin Thompson, *Darkness and Scattered Light,* Garden City, NY: Anchor Books, 1978

St. Nicholai Velimirovic, *The Prologue from Ochrid,* Birmingham, England: Lazarica Press, 1986

Priest Paul Volmensky, "In Memory of the 75th Anniversary of the Murder of Czar Martyr Nicholas II," *Orthodox Life,* Vol. 43, No. 4, July-August 1993

Archimandrite Kallistos Ware and Mother Mary, translators, *The Festal Menaion,* London: Faber & Faber, 1989

Archimandrite Kallistos Ware and Mother Mary, translators, *The Lenten Triodion,* Bussy-en-Othe, France: Monastery of the Veil of the Mother of God, 1979

Timothy (Bishop Kallistos) Ware, *The Orthodox Church,* New York: Penguin Books, 1987

Benjamin D. Williams, "Orthodox Worship: The Orthodox Worship of the Historic Church," *The Christian Activist,* Vol. 3, No. 1, Spring 1992

Ralph L. Woods, editor and compiler, *The World Treasury of Religious Quotations,* New York: Garland Books, 1966

Richard Wurmbrand, "Preparing for the Underground Church," *Epiphany Journal,* Vol. 5, No. 4, Summer 1985

Index

CPSIA information can be obtained
at www.ICGtesting.com
Printed in the USA
BVHW072343200121
598273BV00002B/150